America's Courts on Trial

America's Courts on Trial

Questioning Our Legal System

Elaine Pascoe

Issue and Debate
The Millbrook Press
Brookfield, Connecticut

For M

Photographs courtesy of Reuters/Corbis-Bettmann: pp. 10, 55, 72; Corbis-Bettmann: pp. 16, 70; North Wind Picture Archives: pp. 26, 27; AP/Wide World: pp. 31, 34, 37, 50, 91; SABA: pp. 42 (© Steve Starr), 54, 57; Agence France Presse/Corbis-Bettmann: pp. 49, 88; Miami Herald: p. 59.

Library of Congress Cataloging-in-Publication Data
Pascoe, Elaine.
America's courts on trial: questioning our legal system / Elaine Pascoe.
p.   cm.   (Issue and debate)
Includes bibliographical references and index.
Summary: Examines controversial aspects of America's court system such as whether the concept of trial by jury is out-moded, the courts are racially biased, or media coverage of trials should be limited.
ISBN 0-7613-0104-6 (lib. bdg.)
1. Courts—United States—Juvenile literature. 2. Justice, Administration of—United States—Juvenile literature.
[1. Courts. 2. Justice, Administration of.] I. Title. II. Series.
KF8700.Z9P37 1997 347.73'1—dc21 97-109 CIP AC

Published by The Millbrook Press, Inc.
2 Old New Milford Road
Brookfield, Connecticut 06804

Contents

Introduction
9

Chapter One
America's Courts
13

Chapter Two
Judging the Jury
23

Chapter Three
Race and Justice
41

Chapter Four
Money and Justice
52

Chapter Five
Trial by Television
63

Chapter Six
The Rights of the Defendant
75

Chapter Seven
The Rights of the Victim
85

Chapter Eight
The Trial Game
95

Notes 99
Further Reading 105
Index 107

America's
Courts
on Trial

Introduction

In countries ruled by dictators who permit no opposition,
people live in fear of arrest. At any time, the police may
burst through the door. Anyone can be thrown into prison
for any reason, or for no reason at all. Once in jail, the
prisoner may never get a hearing. Even if there's a trial,
the court will be biased against the accused, and a "guilty"
verdict is certain. In such countries the legal system becomes an instrument of terror, used by the government to
silence dissent.

Americans are protected from this nightmare by the
U.S. Constitution, which guarantees the right to a fair trial.
By law, anyone accused of a crime is entitled to an impartial hearing in court, before a jury made up of average
people. Defendants are assumed to be innocent until the
facts prove otherwise, and they are allowed ample opportunity to prove the charges false. This right is one that
Americans cherish, and it's one of the concepts that, tra-
ditionally, have made them proud of their country.

Today, however, many Americans have begun to question their legal system. No one takes issue with the consti-

*The murder trial of O. J. Simpson brought many of the issues
that plague America's legal system to the forefront of
popular thought and kindled the debate. Simpson was tried
and acquitted of murdering his ex-wife, Nicole Brown
Simpson, pictured here, and her friend Ronald Goldman.*

tutional promise of a fair trial. But there's plenty of debate about whether the current legal system can reliably deliver on the promise and, if not, what should be done to fix the system.

The debate has heated up largely because of a series of highly publicized criminal trials, of which the most famous was the 1995 murder trial of former football star and film actor O. J. Simpson. Simpson was accused of the brutal slaying of his former wife, Nicole Brown Simpson, and her friend Ronald Goldman in Brentwood, California, on June 12, 1994. The Simpson trial, which was televised and trumpeted in the media as the "trial of the century," captured public attention for nine months. By the time the jury delivered a verdict of "not guilty" on October 3, 1995, Americans had been immersed for months in details of the evidence and in the personalities of the judge, the prosecuting and defense attorneys, and the chief witnesses.

Most had also seen far more of an actual criminal court proceeding than they had ever encountered before. In a way, the Simpson trial became a sort of lens through which Americans viewed the legal system. And whether they agreed with the jury's verdict or not, they came face to face with some of the problems that confront courts today. Among those problems are these:

• Is the concept of trial by jury outmoded? Some people contend that many trials today involve legal and technical questions that are too complex for average people to grasp, and that judges and expert arbitrators are better equipped to decide the outcome. The ways in which juries are selected, and the rules under which jury trials are conducted, have also come under fire.

• Are courts racially biased? Those who say "yes" point to statistical evidence showing higher rates of arrest and conviction, and stiffer sentences, for nonwhites. Those who say "no" argue that other factors are at work, and that the legal system merely reflects problems in society as a whole.

• Do courts favor the rich and famous? Judges and juries may not consciously side with wealth, but money buys top-level legal representation and allows defendants to present the strongest possible case. Do poor people have an equal opportunity when they're accused of crimes?

• Should media coverage of trials be limited? Extensive coverage can make a fair trial impossible, some people say, by surrounding the proceedings with a circus atmosphere. Others say that the media help ensure fairness, by keeping the proceedings under close scrutiny.

• Do courts go too far in protecting the rights of defendants? For example, rules that govern the collecting of evidence have been blamed for allowing criminals to walk free. But some people are concerned that easing the rules will weaken individual rights and allow courts and law enforcement agencies to stack the deck against defendants.

• Should courts offer greater recourse to victims of crimes? There's strong popular feeling in favor of this, but some legal scholars worry that focusing on the plight of victims may skew criminal trials, diverting attention from the evidence that should determine the innocence or guilt of the accused.

To better understand the debates that surround these questions, the first step is to take a look at the way the American legal system developed, and how it is designed to work today.

Chapter One

America's Courts

In all criminal prosecutions, the accused shall enjoy the right to a speedy and public trial, by an impartial jury of the State and district wherein the crime shall have been committed . . . .
—Sixth Amendment to the U.S. Constitution

The Sixth Amendment's guarantee of a "speedy and public" jury trial is only one of many constitutional provisions designed to protect people who are accused of crimes or who become caught up in the legal system in some other way—in a civil lawsuit, for example. In fact, five of the ten amendments that make up the Bill of Rights, as well as sections of the original Constitution, deal with the relationship between individuals and law enforcement authorities. These constitutional guarantees provide the underpinnings for the American judicial system, which includes federal, state, and municipal courts.

The provisions in the Constitution offer a clear indication of just how concerned America's founders were about the potential for courts to trample on individual rights. Many of these guarantees reflect principles of law that developed in England and were firmly established long before British colonies were founded in North America. Others were written in by the founders as protection against abuses they believed Americans had suffered at the hands of British authorities in the years leading up to the Revolutionary War.

The Constitutional Guarantees. Article I, section 9, of the Constitution contains one of the most basic principles: the guarantee of habeas corpus. This Latin phrase, literally translated, means "you shall have the body." In legal terms, a writ of habeas corpus requires authorities to bring anyone they arrest before a judge. The judge hears the reasons for the arrest and can release the suspect if those reasons aren't lawful. This guarantee prevents the authorities from holding people in prison unjustly, for personal or political reasons.

The same section of the Constitution prohibits two other potential abuses: bills of attainder and ex post facto laws. A bill of attainder declares someone guilty of a crime without holding a trial. An ex post facto law allows individuals to be tried for actions that were not considered crimes when they were committed.

Article III provides for a federal court system (described later in this chapter) and defines the types of cases federal courts may hear. It also guarantees that anyone accused of a major crime has the right to a trial by jury. As a protection against political persecution, it outlines a narrow and limited definition for the crime of treason.

Only a few other specific individual rights were included in the Constitution as it was written in 1787. When states began the process of debating and approving (ratifying) the document, however, it was soon clear that many people were concerned by this. To win ratification, supporters of the Constitution promised to add a bill of rights, similar to the guarantees of specific rights that had been included in the state constitutions of Virginia, Maryland, and Massachusetts. The result was the U.S. Bill of Rights, ratified in 1791. It includes these provisions:

• The Fourth Amendment prohibits "unreasonable searches and seizures" of people or their property. Authorities must go to court and obtain a warrant before conducting a search. To get the warrant, they must show "probable cause"—a reason why the search is justified. The warrant must describe the person or place to be searched, and state what the authorities hope to find.

• The Fifth Amendment contains one of the core rights in the Constitution: the guarantee that no one can be "deprived of life, liberty, or property, without due process of law." "Due process" includes a fair hearing conducted under established legal procedures, with safeguards that protect individuals against the power of the government. The Fifth Amendment also states that a person can't be brought to trial for a major crime unless a grand jury first hears evidence and presents an indictment, or formal charge; this helps deter officials from bringing groundless charges against individuals. The same amendment prohibits double jeopardy (being retried after an acquittal for the same crime), states that courts can't force individuals to testify against themselves, and requires government to compensate people when their property is taken for public use.

• The Sixth Amendment covers criminal cases—that is, cases in which someone is accused of violating a law. In addition to guaranteeing the right to a prompt, public jury trial, it says that individuals must be informed of the nature of the charges against them and the reasons why

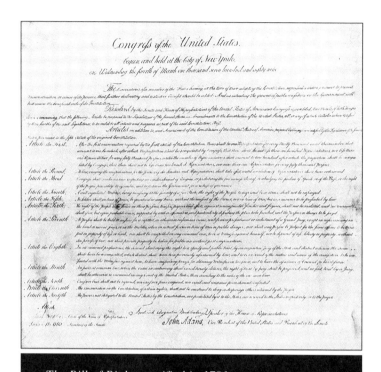

The Bill of Rights, ratified in 1791, guarantees specific rights for Americans, most of them having to do with protection under the law. The framers of the U.S. Constitution promised to add a bill of rights to that document as many people called for at the time the Constitution was written in 1787.

they have been accused. They have the right to be confronted with the witnesses against them, to call defense witnesses and require them to testify, and to have legal counsel.

• The Seventh Amendment extends the right to a trial by jury to civil lawsuits—disputes between individuals, corporations, and other entities. It states that a judge can overturn a jury verdict only on the grounds that the verdict violates legal rules, not on the facts of the case.

• The Eighth Amendment prohibits excessive bail and fines, and cruel and unusual punishments.

At the time the Bill of Rights was adopted, most people viewed its guarantees as restrictions on the federal government. Many state constitutions contained similar guarantees, restricting the actions of state governments. After the Civil War, however, the Constitution was amended again to prevent states from denying rights to newly freed slaves. The Fourteenth Amendment prohibits states from infringing on the rights guaranteed by federal law, including the Constitution, and from denying any person due process or equal protection under the law.

Parallel Court Systems. The organization of the U.S. judicial system reflects the way the country is governed. Just as there are federal, state, and local governments, there are federal, state, and local (municipal) courts. Governments at all levels pass laws and ordinances that prohibit certain acts, from felonies (serious crimes) such as drug trafficking and murder to misdemeanors (minor offenses) such as jaywalking. When a federal law is violated, the case goes to a federal court. Violations of state laws are tried in state courts, and violations of town ordinances are tried in municipal or state courts.

State and federal court systems are parallel—that is, each includes trial courts, where cases originate, and higher courts, where appeals are heard. States use various names for trial courts—they're called circuit courts in Illinois and superior courts in California, for example. Some states have separate courts for civil and criminal cases or for cases involving children. In others, trial courts have general jurisdiction—that is, they can hear any sort of case.

Appeals travel to intermediate appeals courts and from there to the state supreme court.

The lowest level in the federal court system is made up of the federal district courts. Each state has at least one federal district court, and some states have several. Besides criminal cases involving U.S. laws, the federal district courts hear a limited number of civil cases: lawsuits in which the U.S. government is a party, suits between individuals from different states when more than $50,000 is at stake, and cases that involve claims based on federal law, including the Constitution.

A Criminal Case. Here's how a typical criminal case might work its way through the system. Suppose the police identify a man—let's call him John Suspect—whom they believe is behind a string of burglaries. They file a formal sworn complaint with a court official, who issues an arrest warrant for Suspect. (Sometimes the warrant is issued after the actual arrest. In some cases, a district or state attorney submits a document called an information to the court. Like a sworn complaint, this outlines the reasons for believing that an individual committed a crime.) Suspect is arrested, advised of his rights, and booked (meaning the arrest is recorded).

Next, Suspect is arraigned in court. He hears the specific charges and enters a plea: not guilty, guilty, or nolo contendere ("I will not contest it," in Latin; the accused doesn't argue that he's innocent, but he doesn't actually admit guilt, either). If he can't afford to hire a lawyer, the court will appoint a public defender to represent him. A plea of guilty or nolo contendere would be followed by sentencing; but Suspect pleads not guilty, so the case continues. The court may order him to be held in jail or may release him on payment of bail, money held as security to ensure that he will show up for his next court date.

That date will most likely be for a preliminary hearing. The purpose of this hearing is to determine that a crime was committed and that there are reasonable grounds to think that Suspect was involved. State prosecutors present the evidence that they've gathered against him, but he has no opportunity to present witnesses or argue his side of the case. If the judge thinks the evidence is insufficient, the case will be dismissed. But in this case that doesn't happen, and the judge orders it to trial.

Some criminal cases go to trial by a different route: A grand jury, made up of six to thirty average citizens, is selected and meets to decide whether there's enough evidence to proceed. The grand jury can hear evidence presented by prosecutors, but it can also open its own investigation and call its own witnesses. Grand jury proceedings are usually secret, to protect innocent people who may become involved in the investigations. If the grand jury finds enough evidence, it hands up an indictment—a formal charge—to the court.

The court sets a trial date, giving prosecutors and the defense time to prepare their cases. Pretrial hearings may be held to determine whether evidence has been properly obtained and will be admissible in court. At any time, even during the trial itself, Suspect can decide to change his plea. He may also plea-bargain—strike a deal with prosecutors in which he pleads guilty to a lesser charge, accepting a lighter penalty and sparing the state the trouble of going to trial.

If Suspect doesn't decide to bargain, the trial begins with the selection of the jury, twelve men and women who will decide his guilt or innocence. (See Chapter 2 for more about the jury selection process.) The judge presides over the trial and decides all questions that arise about evidence, procedure, and interpretation of the law. It's the jury's job to determine the facts. When the jury is impaneled (selected), the prosecuting and defense attorneys deliver opening statements, outlining what they plan to prove during the trial. Then the prosecution presents its case against the defendant. Suspect's lawyers have a chance to cross-examine the prosecution witnesses; then they present their case, and the prosecution cross-examines. Each side sums up in closing arguments, the judge instructs the jury on the applicable principles of law, and the jury retires to consider the evidence. A "not guilty" verdict will set Suspect free immediately. If the jury can't make up its mind, the judge will be forced to declare a mistrial. The prosecution will have to decide whether to charge Suspect again and go ahead with a second trial.

In this case, though, the jury returns a verdict of "guilty." It signals the start of what may be a series of legal proceedings. Rather than handing down a sentence on the spot, the judge schedules a separate sentencing hearing. Suspect, meanwhile, decides to appeal the verdict at the next level in the judicial system, the state appeals court.

Appeals court judges review cases without calling witnesses or accepting evidence, so they rarely overturn a verdict on the facts—they assume that the trial jury was best informed to decide what actually happened. Successful appeals are usually made on the grounds of errors in procedure or misinterpretation of the law. Perhaps, for example, the trial judge in Suspect's case allowed the prosecution to present evidence that had been illegally obtained. Or perhaps the judge gave unclear instructions to the jury about legal principles. If the appeal is unsuccessful, Suspect's lawyers may decide to carry it to the state supreme court. Or, if they think questions of federal law or constitutional rights are involved, they may appeal in federal court. The U.S. Supreme Court hears only cases appealed from state supreme courts and from federal appeals courts. It can decide which cases to hear, and the roughly 170 cases the Supreme Court handles each year are just a fraction of the number it's asked to review.

A Civil Case. In a civil case, the issue is a dispute between parties, not the violation of a law. The parties may be individuals, corporations, even government agencies. They may be seeking money for damages they believe they have suffered; a court order (such as an injunction, which forbids specific behavior); or a decree, such as a divorce. Most civil cases begin in state courts, and they follow the same routes on appeals that criminal cases take.

Here's how a civil case might proceed. Suppose that, after twenty years with a company, a fifty-five-year-old sales manager—we'll call her Jane Quota—is laid off from her job. The company says it's cutting its work force and eliminating the sales manager's job; but, a few months later, it hires a thirty-five-year-old "sales supervisor" to do essentially the same work. The sales manager believes she has been discriminated against on the basis of age. She consults an attorney, who agrees to represent her. Quota files suit against the company, demanding reinstatement in her job, back pay, and compensation for her legal expenses.

Because both state and federal laws prohibit discrimination in employment on the basis of age, Quota can bring her case in either a state or a federal court. She takes the federal route, but it's a long one. Pretrial proceedings drag on and on, as each side prepares its case and then, through a process called discovery, reviews the evidence that the other side intends to present. The court calendar is crowded, but, finally, a date is set. But the defense hasn't completed its case, and the case is postponed, or, in legal terms, continued.

At any time during this process, the two sides can agree to an out-of-court settlement. The employer might agree to pay Quota a lump sum, for example, while in exchange she agrees to drop her suit. If there's no settlement, the case goes to trial. The defendant (the employer, in this case) can waive the right to a trial by jury and let the judge decide the matter. That makes sense when a judge is likely to be more sympathetic than a jury made up of average people. Whoever decides the case, the losing side can appeal the verdict or the amount of any award granted by the trial court. By the time the process is finally finished, years may have passed.

More than time may be wasted in pursuing a civil lawsuit through the courts. It's expensive to sue—legal fees, filing fees, and other costs can add up to thousands of dollars. In many cases, even winning the suit doesn't bring an award large enough to cover the costs in terms of money, time, and worry. As a rule, poor and most middle-class people simply can't afford to sue, unless an attorney agrees to take the case on a contingency basis (that is, with no fee unless damages are recovered). Filing a lawsuit isn't a realistic option for many Americans, even though the large number of cases clogging the system would suggest otherwise.

The cost of civil justice is a serious problem for the American legal system. In this book, our focus is mainly on the problems that arise in handling criminal cases. In those cases, too, wealth sometimes appears to be an advantage. That is just one of the imbalances that, some people argue, plague the system.

Chapter Two

Judging the Jury

We swear in juries composed of fools and rascals, because the system rigidly excludes honest men and men of brains.[1]

—Mark Twain

After hearing testimony and arguments for nine long months, the jury in the O. J. Simpson murder trial returned its verdict after less than three hours of deliberation—and set off a storm of controversy. Not just the verdict or the speed with which it was reached, but the American jury system itself, came under fire. Sophisticated legal maneuvering, tensions in society, the sheer length of some trials, and other factors make it impossible for juries today to reach impartial verdicts, some critics said. Others found the system flawed to the core. "The American jury system does not work to free the innocent and punish the guilty in an efficient and humane manner," wrote one commentator. "It never has."[2]

The jury's role has evolved since the founding of the nation, and juries today often face daunting pressures and challenges. Yet much about the jury system—much that's good, as well as much that isn't—has hardly changed in hundreds of years.

How the System Began. Because the right to trial by jury is guaranteed in the Constitution, many people consider it part and parcel of a democratic society, like the right to vote. In fact, the jury system developed quite separately, and from a very different source, than the democratic tradition that began in ancient Greece. The idea of a twelve-person jury probably originated with the Vikings of Scandinavia and was carried by them to England in the early Middle Ages.

In the court system set up by Anglo-Saxon English rulers, however, the jury's role was not what it is today. Each district court appointed a group of twelve men, all leading landowners, who swore an oath to neither shield the guilty nor accuse the innocent. The main job of these "lawmen" was to arrest wrongdoers and bring them to court, but in at least some cases they also passed judgment. Guilt was determined in ways we find bizarre today. The accused and accuser (or their champions) might fight it out, on the theory that heaven would grant the victory to the party that was right. Or the accused might be put through an ordeal—held underwater, for example— in the belief that innocents would be protected from harm. In a third sort of trial, the defendant made his case in court and swore to it. Rather than backing up his word with evidence, he produced "oath-helpers," witnesses and neighbors who swore that his oath was pure and true. The number of oath-helpers required depended on the nature of the case and the social standing of the witness (the word of a nobleman or a church official carried more weight than the word of a commoner). If enough stepped forward, the defendant won the case.[3]

The English jury system developed out of the Anglo-Saxon tradition of lawmen and oath-helpers. By the 1300s jurors were neither arresting officers nor witnesses. Instead, their main job was to hear evidence and decide the outcome of the case. And by the 1600s, trial by jury was firmly established as part of English common law. Judges decided all questions of law, including whether a crime had been committed and what sort of arguments could be presented in court. Juries decided the basic facts: Did the defendant commit the act in question? Jurors were expected to be impartial and base their decisions on evidence and testimony, not just on personal knowledge of the case.

Still, jury verdicts were often influenced, and sometimes even forced, by the government. Jurors who refused to vote with the majority (thus preventing the jury from reaching a unanimous verdict) might be punished. That began to change in 1670, when William Penn and William Mead were put on trial in London for the crime of preaching in the streets. The jury deadlocked—four jurors refused to vote to convict the men. Court officials arrested the stubborn jurors, and they were fined and thrown in jail. But the jurors went back to court and won. If jurors could be ordered to vote a certain way, the judge who heard their petition wrote, "the jury is but a troublesome delay, a great charge, and of no use." His ruling marked a turning point: Jurors could no longer be punished for their verdicts.[4]

Juries in Early America. Trial by jury was a fundamental right to the British colonists who settled in North America in the 1600s and 1700s. And when American colonists began to clash with British authorities, juries started to play an increasingly important role in protect-

THE
New - York Weekly JOURNAL.

Containing the freſheſt Advices, Foreign, and Domeſtick.

MUNDAY January 27th, 1734.

Juſtum et tenacem propoſiti Virum,
Non civium Ardor prava jubentium,
Non Vultus inſtantis Tyranni,
Mente quatit ſolida.

Hor.

THE firſt eſſential Ingredient Neceſſary to form a Patriot, is Impartiality; for if a Perſon ſhall think himſelf bound by any other Rules but thoſe of his own Reaſon and Judgment, or obliged to follow the Dictates of others, who ſhall appear the Heads of the Party he is ingaged in, he ſinks below the Dignity of a Humane Creature, and voluntarily reſigns thoſe Guides which Nature has given him, to direct him in all Spheres of Life.

The Coldneſs, and ſometimes Diſdain, which a Man governed thus by the Principles of Honour generally meets with on ſuch Occaſions from the Friends he has ever acted in Concert with, for the former Part of his Life, are Conſiderations which but too often ſubdue the beſt inclined Spirits, and prevail with them to be paſſive and obedient, rather than active and reſolute : But if ſuch Perſons could but once feel the Comfort and Pleaſure of having done their Duty, they would meet with a ſufficient Reward within themſelves, to over ballance the Loſs of their Friends, or the Malice of their Enemies.

Ambition and Avarice are two Vices, which are directly oppoſite to the Character of a Patriot, for tho' an Increaſe of Power, or of Riches, may be the proper Reward of Honour and Merit, and the moſt honeſt Stateſman may, with Juſtice accept of either ; yet when the Mind is infected with a Thirſt after them, all Notions of Truth, Principle and Independency are Loſt in ſuch Minds, and, by growing Slaves to their own Paſſions, they become Naturally ſubſervient to thoſe who can indulge and gratify them.

In public Affairs it is the Duty of every Man to be free from perſonal Prejudices ; neither ought we to oppoſe any Step that is taking for the Good of our Country, purely becauſe thoſe that are the Contrivers and Adviſers of it, are Obnoxious to us. There are but too many Precedents of this Nature, when Men have caſt the moſt black Colours on the Wiſeſt of Adminiſtrations, becauſe thoſe that had the Direction of Affairs were their Enemies in private Life ; and this ill Way of Judging may be attended with dangerous Conſequences to the common Weal.

Intrepidity and Firmneſs are two Virtues which every Patriot muſt be Maſter of, or elſe all the other Talents he is poſſeſs'd of are uſeleſs and barren.

Whoever, therefore, when he has form'd a Judgment on any Subject relating

John Peter Zenger's publication of a defamatory article (facing page) about the British governor of New York resulted in a landmark trial in 1735 in which the groundwork for free speech was laid. It was also important to the development of the jury system in this country.

ing those who criticized the government. The first step in that direction came in 1735, in the trial of John Peter Zenger, the publisher of the *New-York Weekly Journal.*

Zenger had been arrested and jailed for printing material critical of New York's British governor, William Cosby. The judges at his trial ruled that the *Weekly Journal*'s criticisms of Cosby did, in fact, violate the law, that they were "seditious libel"—defamatory statements that undermined the authority of the government. Since Zenger freely admitted that he had published the material, it seemed clear that the jury could only find him guilty. But Zenger's lawyer, Andrew Hamilton of Philadelphia, argued that the statements in the newspaper did not violate the law because they were true. Citizens, he said, had a right to criticize the government if their statements were not false or malicious. When the judges would not hear this defense, Hamilton turned to the jurors and presented the argument to them directly, urging them to interpret the law in Zenger's favor. They did, and found Zenger not guilty.

The Zenger trial was a landmark in the development of free speech in America, but it was also important to the development of the jury system. The jury in the case broke new ground by ruling on the law, not just the facts of the case, and doing so to protect an individual against government authority. The Zenger verdict didn't change the colonial justice system. But by the time of the Revolutionary War, the idea that a jury made up of average citizens could serve as a buffer against authority was widely held. It was no wonder, then, that the right to trial by jury was set out in the Constitution, linked to America's democratic form of government.

Until after the Civil War, it was fairly common for juries to deliver verdicts that seemed to fly in the face of the law. For example, because the Constitution requires states to honor other states' laws, northern courts were supposed to return fugitive slaves to the South. But when these cases went to trial, northern juries often refused to do so.

By the late 1800s, however, courts were beginning to set limits on the power of juries to overrule the law, a power known as jury nullification. Some states allowed trial judges to order juries to free defendants in criminal cases when legal grounds required acquittal. Some gave judges the final say in civil cases. In 1896 the U.S. Supreme Court ruled that juries in federal courts could decide only the facts of a case and had to accept the judge's ruling on the law.

Still, in the eyes of most Americans, even within these limits the jury trial has remained a bulwark against injustice and a key component of democracy. That hasn't prevented legal scholars and others from pointing out flaws in the system, however. Juror selection is one of the greatest areas of concern.

The Jury Pool. The selection process begins with a jury pool—a group of citizens who are called for jury duty. With only the most basic requirements for service—citizenship, literacy in English, no criminal record—jury pools might be expected to reflect the community, including people with various jobs and levels of income, different backgrounds, and different levels of education. In practice, that's often not the case. In many areas fewer than half the people who are called for duty actually show up in court.[5] In some cases, they've moved away and the summons doesn't reach them. But many just throw the summons away. Jury service is mandatory in federal courts, but state rules vary, and enforcement is often lax.

Even when prospective jurors obey the summons, many are excused from serving. People in certain occupations—firefighters, police officers, public officials—are automatically excused; others, including physicians, are often excused because of the importance of their work. Many other people plead hardships of one kind or another: work conflicts, illnesses, and so on. Juries often have a high percentage of retirees, simply because they're available to serve, and a low percentage of businesspeople and professionals.

Voir Dire. At the start of a trial, a number of people are chosen at random from the pool to be considered for the jury of that trial. In a process called voir dire (Anglo-French for "to speak the truth"), the prospective jurors are quizzed by the trial judge and usually by the lawyers representing both sides of the case. Jurors who might be biased—because they know people involved in the case, for example, or have already formed an opinion about it—are "challenged for cause" and turned down. Prosecution and defense attorneys may also dismiss a limited number of potential jurors without giving any reason, using what is called a peremptory challenge. (In most states, lawyers are allowed two or three such challenges in civil cases to as many as twenty-five in capital cases, where the death penalty is a possibility.) In this way, each side can eliminate jurors who may be hostile to its case.

The goal of the voir dire process is to ensure that jurors are impartial and rational, able to draw their own conclusions from the evidence that they'll hear in court. But critics of the jury system point out that the result is often quite the opposite: a jury that is poorly equipped to review evidence and predisposed toward one side or the other. Judges and attorneys alike are at fault, they say.

Potential jurors enter the U.S. district court house in Manhattan in 1993. A number of them were marked for possible participation in the trial of the World Trade Center bombers. The present jury system is constantly under attack, and many reforms have been suggested.

Judges often eliminate people who have heard media reports about the case, on the grounds that this may have led them to form opinions about the case before they review the facts. But people who read newspapers and follow the news tend to be among the better-educated and better-informed members of society. If a judge is too cautious and eliminates everyone who has heard even a snippet of news about the case, the jury may be made up of people who don't know very much about anything. This isn't a new problem; in his 1871 book *Roughing It,* Mark Twain described a murder trial in which the judge excluded all prospective jurors who had read news of the case. In the court's view, he concluded, "Ignoramuses alone could mete out unsullied justice."[6]

What is new is the length to which lawyers go in the effort to shape juries that will be sympathetic to their cases or, especially if the case is a weak one, easily confused. Stephen J. Adler, a newspaper editor who has written extensively on jury reform, notes: "Many of those who are currently removed via lawyers' challenges appear to be more alert and unbiased than many who are seated."[7]

While lawyers have long used the peremptory challenge to exclude potential jurors who may be unsympathetic, until recently they acted on hunches, using instinct and experience to decide whether to include an individual or not. Now many lawyers turn to jury consultants to help make the choice. Jury consulting is a new profession that has blossomed since the late 1970s. Consultants use the tools of marketing and politics, including polls and focus groups, to help shape the outcome of trials. Polls determine what types of people may be sympathetic or hostile. This helps lawyers select jurors. Focus groups, made up of individuals with backgrounds similar to those of the jurors, allow lawyers to try out various tactics and gauge what the jury's reaction may be. This helps them present their case in the most effective way. In some cases, attorneys have seated a "shadow jury" in the audience of the courtroom. The shadow jury, a group that mirrors the makeup of the actual jury, can give the lawyers daily feedback, allowing them to fine-tune their presentations.

Some jury consultants claim remarkable success rates. One of the consultants used by the defense in the Simpson trial, for example, reportedly succeeded in picking favorable juries in ninety out of one hundred cases.[8] And the Simpson case "was over with the jury pick," one trial consultant said. "It's not that this jury would never convict Simpson, but that they were open to theories" that the police set him up, as the defense would later contend in court.[9] Some legal experts think that the work of jury consultants is overrated, since consultants are apt to take credit in cases where the evidence would have led any jury to vote the same way. Still, even prosecutors are turning to consultants for help in choosing juries that will favor their side. Prosecutors in the Simpson case were criticized for rejecting the advice of a consultant they had retained.

The ability of lawyers to handpick juries that will vote their way has many people concerned. If the jury is biased before the trial begins, how can the verdict be fair? And how can people have confidence in the system? Adler asks, "Why should we defer to the decision of a group of individuals who have been selected for their likely partisanship and then persuaded by many of the same techniques that sell soap and breakfast cereal?"[10]

The Jury in Court. It's not surprising that many people consider jury duty a hardship and go out of their way to avoid it. Jurors are compensated, but the pay ($5 to $50 a day, depending on the state) is barely enough to cover expenses like carfare and child care. A trial may be over quickly or last weeks—or months. During that time, ju-

(33)

Jurors in the 1951 espionage trial of Morton Sobell and Julius and Ethel Rosenberg board a bus after they were ordered sequestered for the night by the presiding judge. Some feel that sequestration, especially for long periods of time, adversely affects the deliberations of juries.

rors are forbidden to discuss the case among themselves or with others. In high-profile cases, they may be sequestered, or confined, to shield them from contact with the public and with media reports about the case. Sequestration may mean a short hotel stay, but on occasion it's a real hardship. In the Simpson trial, the jury was sequestered for more than eight months, from January 24 to October 3. The long sequestration contributed to tensions between the jurors and court officials, and some critics suggested it was a factor in the speed with which the jurors returned a verdict.

Moreover, long and complex trials can be challenging for jurors. They listen as the prosecution and defense present evidence, question witnesses, and argue their cases. But in nearly all states, jurors themselves can't ask questions. Most lawyers and judges believe they should not. Jurors, they say, are likely to ask improper questions— for example, they may mention matters that the judge has already decided must be excluded from the trial. But not being able to ask questions makes it harder for jurors to follow confusing testimony and understand complex evidence. Arizona has begun an experimental program that allows jurors to submit written questions to the trial judge, who screens them before posing them in court. Elsewhere, however, the jury's role is still passive. Some judges even forbid note-taking, although it's increasingly common for jurors to jot down notes about the proceedings.

Some critics of the jury system argue that even a group of capable and unbiased citizens may be overwhelmed by complex court proceedings. Like many other complaints about the jury system, this isn't new. In 1603 a British judge refused to let a jury decide a complex case, ruling that he was better able to judge than "a jury of ploughmen."[11] In civil as well as criminal cases today, juries are often faced with mountains of complicated and technical evidence. In one civil case, jurors listened to twenty-three witnesses and eighty-five depositions over a seven-month period, and the trial record filled 108 volumes. Keeping track of who said what would have been hard even if they had been allowed to take notes, which they weren't.[12] In addition to digesting volumes of evidence, average citizens today may be asked to rule in matters that involve high finance, electronics, cutting-edge forensic science, and other areas where most people have little knowledge. Expert testimony may help make the facts clear, shoot right over the jurors' heads, or confuse matters as defense and prosecution experts present conflicting opinions. When juries are overwhelmed or can't grasp the facts of a case, critics contend, they're likely to follow their emotions when they vote. The same thing may happen when jurors don't understand the law.

Whether fault lies with the system itself or with individual juries, judges, or manipulative lawyers, controversial verdicts have underscored the problem. In one highly publicized criminal case, two juries were unable to reach a verdict in the joint murder trial of Erik and Lyle Menendez, brothers who brutally murdered their wealthy parents in 1993. The brothers admitted the shotgun slayings but claimed they were justified because their father had abused them. (The Menendez brothers were convicted in a second trial.) In civil cases, juries have sometimes awarded extraordinary sums on what seem to be very thin grounds. In a 1992 case, an Alabama jury awarded $4 million to a physician who sued the German automaker BMW when he learned that his new car had been repainted after leaving the factory. In 1994 a McDonald's customer was awarded $2.9 million after she

The murder trial of Lyle (left) and Erik Menendez was highly publicized, and resulted in a hung jury. The emotional testimony of the brothers contributed to the jury's inability to reach a verdict. The Menendez brothers were later convicted in a second trial.

spilled hot coffee on herself and was burned at one of the company's restaurants. (In both cases, the defendants appealed, and the awards were significantly reduced by appeals court judges.)

The Verdict on the Jury. Controversial verdicts like these make good fuel for critics of the jury system. Some observers suggest that juries are nothing more than a relic from the Middle Ages, and that courts might be better off if their role was limited—or eliminated. They point out that the United States conducts more jury trials than any other nation, about 160,000 annually in state and federal courts.[13] Unlike the United States, which bases its criminal justice system on English common law, most Western democracies follow a tradition that goes back to ancient Rome. In this so-called civil-law tradition, juries are used only in certain kinds of trials. Even then, juries are small and made up of professional judges, who are skilled in reviewing evidence, and lay judges, who act as a check on professionals.

Changing to such a system might restore credibility to U.S. trial courts, critics argue. "We can begin by admitting that some of the foreigners who look aghast at spectacles like the Simpson trial actually may have something to teach us about devising a criminal justice system capable of telling right from wrong," wrote one.[14] But it's not likely that most Americans will give up their cherished right to trial by jury—nor is it clear that they should. "A defendant's right to trial by jury in a criminal case remains one of our people's strongest protections against tyranny; the government can't keep any of us behind bars unless it convinces a jury to do so," says Stephen Adler. "The jury system can be saved and is, for all our disappointments, well worth saving."[15] Here are some of the reforms that have been proposed:

• Broaden jury pools. For example, drawing names from driver's license lists rather than voter registration lists will bring in more young people and poor people, many of whom drive but aren't registered to vote.

• Require service, and limit exclusions. To truly get a cross section of society, some critics argue, jury service must be mandatory, with penalties for those who dodge it and exceptions granted only in extreme cases. Limiting exclusions will bring more educated professionals and businesspeople into the pool.

• Make reporting for jury duty less painful. Many states are already attempting to do this. For example, in some states, prospective jurors may need to show up in court only once, rather than checking in daily for up to a month. If they aren't picked to serve on a jury that day, their service is done.

• Streamline jury selection by allowing the judge, but not the attorneys, to question prospective jurors, which would end or limit peremptory challenges. This would go a long way toward ending attorneys' efforts to pick "friendly" jurors. The United States would not be the first country to eliminate peremptory challenges; Britain did so in 1988. Jurors there are now chosen by the luck of the draw. They may be excluded "for cause" by the judge, but lawyers don't question them. The jury selection process takes minutes, rather than the days and weeks it often takes in the United States.

• Make trials shorter and more "juror-friendly": Judges can limit the time spent presenting evidence, bar repetitive testimony, and keep proceedings moving along by minimizing interruptions. Some courts have appointed special officials to help jurors solve problems that crop up during their service. Jurors should be sequestered only when it's absolutely necessary.

• Involve the jury: Allow jurors to take notes and submit questions to the judge, who can ask the questions after consulting with the prosecution and defense attorneys. Lawyers might also give interim summaries in long trials, to help jurors keep track of the proceedings.

Many of these reforms can be put in place by individual courts, and some legal experts believe they may be all that's needed to bring the time-honored tradition of the jury into the twenty-first century. "When people are upset with the outcome in a particular case, there's a temptation to tinker with the system," one judge remarked in the aftermath of the Simpson verdict. "The system isn't perfect, but we have to be careful about removing long-term rights and protections because we don't like what has happened in one instance."[16]

Chapter
Three
Race and
Justice

*Not only did we play the race card, we dealt it
from the bottom of the deck.*[1]
  —Simpson defense attorney Robert Shapiro,
     in an ABC television interview
     on October 3, 1995.

On April 29, 1992, rioting broke out in Los Angeles, California. The riots quickly snowballed into some of the worst
in American history, five days of violence in which fifty-
two people were killed, four thousand were injured, and
damage to property reached $850 million. Nearly twelve
thousand people had been arrested by the time police and
federal troops brought the situation under control. The
cause of this violent eruption: a "not guilty" verdict in the
trial of four white Los Angeles police officers who were
accused of beating Rodney King, a black motorist.

Fast-forward three and a half years to Los Angeles in
October 1995, when the "not guilty" verdict in the Simpson
trial was announced. Many African Americans cheered
the acquittal, and some celebrated openly in the streets.

The issue of race and justice was bitterly felt after the "not guilty" verdict in the Rodney King beating trial in 1992. Days of rioting and looting ensued, as well as more constructive demonstrations by African Americans and others demanding justice.

Most whites reacted with dropped jaws; convinced of Simpson's guilt, they found it hard to believe that the jury in the case thought otherwise.

The two cases underscore one of the most serious problems facing American courts: the issue of race. Justice is supposed to be color-blind, but race is an undercurrent that runs throughout the criminal justice system. Racial issues, some people believe, affect everything from arrests to sentences. Minorities, African Americans in particular, can't get fair treatment in court, they say. Others disagree; they say that the system only reflects broader inequalities in society. But even if they're right, the perception of injustice is a very serious problem for the court system.

What the Numbers Say. Statistics tell part of the story. Studies show that growing numbers of young black men are imprisoned or on probation or parole. As of 1995, fully a third of African-American men in their twenties were under the control of the criminal justice system nationally. A 1996 study showed that in California, the percentage was almost 40 percent, compared with just 5 percent of white men in their twenties. At the time, African Americans made up just 7 percent of California's population but accounted for 32 percent of prisoners.[2]

Experts don't agree on what the statistics mean, however. Some see the figures as clear evidence that African Americans are treated differently. In some cases there is discrimination or harassment, they say. This charge was at the core of the case against the police officers who stopped Rodney King after a high-speed chase. A witness videotaped the officers kicking King and hitting him repeatedly with their batons, continuing to do so when he was on the ground. Even before this incident, an investigation into the Los Angeles police department had shown that many officers had poor attitudes about race.

The videotape made the evening news and was aired again and again in the weeks leading up to the trial. Most people who saw it, black and white, felt certain that the policemen would be convicted. They responded with shock and outrage when the jury voted for acquittal. The jurors accepted the defense position—that the officers had been justified in using force because they feared King might attack them. But some people charged that racism was behind the verdict as well as the beating: To avoid publicity, the trial had been held in Simi Valley, a mostly white suburb of Los Angeles. There were no African Americans on the jury.

Even if policemen, judges, and prosecutors don't set out to discriminate against minorities, the system often seems to be stacked against African Americans, some experts argue. Drug laws, and the way they are enforced, provide an example. Penalties are often stiffer for use of crack cocaine than for many other illegal drugs because of crack's association with violence and crime. Under federal law, for instance, the minimum sentence for possessing a pound (half a kilogram) of powdered cocaine is the same as that for possessing just 2 ounces (56 grams) of crack. And the overwhelming majority of defendants in federal crack cases are black, whereas a larger percentage of defendants in powdered cocaine and other drug cases are white, Hispanic, or Asian. But in 1996 the U.S. Supreme Court ruled that such statistics alone don't show discrimination. To prove bias, it would be necessary to show that the government was prosecuting black crack users while "similarly situated defendants of other races could have been prosecuted, but were not."[3]

Other anticrime measures often have their strongest effects in inner-city neighborhoods, too. Does this reflect bias, or patterns of crime? "Conscious or not, it is difficult to imagine the war on crime being waged with this vehemence if middle-class white males were similarly affected," says Vincent Schiraldi, director of the group that conducted the 1996 California study.[4] But other experts disagree. "If you set aside the arrests for crack cocaine, [the figures] are not the result of bias in the criminal justice system," according to one criminologist. "The system is more or less putting people in prison at the rate at which they commit crimes." Solving the problem will require broad social change, to "try to profoundly change the circumstances of people in their early years of life."[5]

Race and the Jury. Once they're caught up in the criminal justice system, members of minority groups often feel that they're treated more harshly than whites—that it's harder for minorities to be released without bail, and that prosecutors are less likely to reduce charges for them. Statistics don't always bear out these allegations, but several factors help create them. While minorities make up a high percentage of defendants, they're often underrepresented in the ranks of judges and prosecuting attorneys. And in many cases, they're underrepresented on juries, too.

Until the 1960s, jury pools often reflected a narrow segment of society. On the theory that only those with high integrity and intelligence should serve, courts sought out leading citizens for jury duty. These so-called key men were generally white men. Women were routinely excused from jury duty, and minorities were routinely excluded. Although the Supreme Court ruled in 1880 that states could not bar African Americans from jury duty by law, nothing stopped state courts from simply not selecting African Americans.

The civil rights movement of the 1950s and 1960s brought change. African Americans, struggling to gain equal rights, argued that all-white juries were often biased against black defendants. In 1968, Congress passed a law that prevented federal courts from excluding jurors on the basis of color, race, sex, national origin, religion, or economic status. The law required jury pools to be chosen at random, to reflect a "fair cross-section of the community."[6]

In 1975, striking down a Louisiana law that exempted women from jury duty, the Supreme Court extended the requirement to state courts. As a result, states expanded their jury pools, drawing on voter registration records and other mass lists. But in many areas minorities still aren't well represented in jury pools. One reason, according to some reports, is that minorities are more likely to ignore jury summonses, because many mistrust the system and because many are poor and simply can't afford to serve without pay.

Even when minorities are in the jury pool, they may not serve on juries. A 1986 Supreme Court ruling barred prosecutors from rejecting jurors on racial grounds, and the ruling was later extended to civil trials and to defense attorneys. In 1994 the court ruled that jurors could not be turned down on the grounds of gender. But race and gender still play major roles in jury selection, critics of the system say. Alvin Alschuler, a University of Chicago law professor and an expert on the jury system, noted soon after the Simpson verdict: "In theory, you're not supposed to take race and gender into account. In practice, it's hard to enforce those rules."[7] Attorneys can often trot out another reason—and almost any other reason will do—for excluding a minority or female juror.

Race and the Verdict. Must a jury be racially balanced to return a fair verdict? It shouldn't be so. In theory, every citizen called for jury duty should weigh the evidence and decide the case based simply on the facts. Yet there are examples of racially biased verdicts throughout American history. "From independence until the civil rights revolution, the jury was a means by which white bigots legally lynched Indians, African Americans, and Asians (or acquitted their white murderers)," notes one commentator. One of the most notorious cases occurred in 1955, when Emmett Till, a black Chicago teenager, was murdered in Mississippi while visiting family; an all-white jury refused to convict the two white men who were his killers. Yet, continues this writer, "Today urban black juries all too often put race above justice in the same manner."[8]

Supporting that view are statistics showing that black defendants in felony cases are acquitted more often in urban areas with large black populations. For example, the national average for acquittals in all felony cases is about 17 percent; black defendants in the Bronx are acquitted at nearly three times that rate.[9] It's not clear whether race or other factors are behind the statistics, but many legal experts acknowledge that race plays a role in at least some acquittals. One school of thought holds that there's a rough sort of justice in this: that African Americans, after years of unequal treatment in the hands of the system, are entitled to turn the tables. Paul Butler, who teaches law at George Washington University in Washington, D.C., sees this as a form of jury nullification, a way of canceling unjust laws. Black jurors, he argued in a 1995 law journal article, are justified in refusing to convict black defendants whom they know are guilty, as a way of countering a system that is stacked against them.[10]

Butler advocated this action only in cases of nonviolent crimes, including drug offenses. But the same philosophy has emerged in court during several high-profile murder cases, including the Simpson trial. In fact, Simpson's defense team was widely criticized for playing the "race card" by arguing that Simpson was framed by racist white detectives. A recording of one detective making racist remarks was a key part of the defense case. Johnnie Cochran, the African-American attorney who played a leading role in Simpson's defense, urged the predominantly black jury to "do the right thing" and use the verdict to send a message about the system. "Cochran implicitly suggested that truth was not paramount," wrote one observer, and "that the prosecution's case was less important than the fact that black people are framed in this country every day."[11]

Other experts say that the role of race is vastly overstated. Whites on the Simpson jury also voted for acquittal, they note. And African Americans have voted to convict black defendants in other high-profile cases. For example, three African Americans were on the jury that convicted boxer Mike Tyson of rape in a sensational case. "It's the height of racism to say that black people, because a defendant is black, will tend to acquit," says Earl Strayhorn, a Chicago judge who has presided over a thousand jury trials. In fact, notes jury expert Alvin Alschuler, most African-American jurors do vote to convict black defendants when the evidence is there. "But most isn't the issue." he adds. "It only takes a few to prevent conviction, and it doesn't have to happen in every case before it becomes troublesome."[12]

Race-based verdicts are disturbing, no matter which way they cut. When juries let violent criminals go free,

Detective Mark Fuhrman of the Los Angeles Police Department was a key witness for the prosecution in the O. J. Simpson trial. Later, he was targeted by the defense as one of the main conspirators in an effort to frame Simpson for the double murder.

A predominantly African-American gathering in South Central Los Angeles celebrates after the announcement of the "not guilty" verdict in the O. J. Simpson case. The widely varied reactions to the verdict revealed a grave difference in the way people perceive justice.

people of all races are at risk. And such verdicts reveal deep divisions in American society. If jurors do, in fact, put racial solidarity ahead of justice, then the gulf between the races is wide indeed.

Whose Justice? The Simpson verdict revealed deep fractures in American society. African Americans and whites read the same newspaper accounts of the trial and watched the same television coverage, and yet they came away with opinions that were radically opposed. Whites who were convinced of Simpson's guilt shook their heads in disbelief at the "not guilty" verdict and talked about the mountain of evidence presented at the trial—evidence that they felt argued clearly for conviction. They felt frustrated, some even angry, that a killer had gone free. Justice had not been done. African Americans who were elated by the verdict pointed to holes in the evidence, including sloppy police procedures, and talked about other cases in which police had manufactured cases against innocent people. For some, this case meant a great deal. With all the publicity that surrounded his trial, Simpson had come to stand for all African-American men, and his acquittal was just.

Perhaps the opinions differed so sharply because they were based not only on facts but also on personal experience and on different community standards. That in itself isn't a bad thing, some observers believe. "Juries were created not to insulate the courtroom from community attitudes but, quite the opposite, to bring community standards in," argues journalist Clarence Page.[13]

But in this case, personal experience and community standards seem to vary so widely that they produce, in effect, two competing views of justice. And a society that can't agree on justice clearly is deeply troubled.

Chapter Four
Money and Justice

Reason and reflection require us to recognize that in our adversary system of criminal justice, any person haled into court who is too poor to hire a lawyer cannot be assured a fair trial unless counsel is provided for him.[1]
—Supreme Court Justice Hugo L. Black

If there is bias in the American justice system, some people believe, it's not directed solely against minorities. Wealth, fame, and connections give some defendants advantages that poor people, even average people, can't hope to obtain. Indeed, as journalist Clarence Page noted after the Simpson trial, part of the joy that some African Americans felt over the verdict stemmed from the "sheer exhilaration they felt at the sight of a rich black man able, for a change, to buy the high quality 'dream team' defense that rich white guys have always taken for granted."[2]

Yet the idea that wealth can influence the outcome of a court case seems to run counter to the constitutional guarantee of a fair trial. How important is money in the

American legal system, and what does its role say about that system?

Rich and Poor. Those who believe that money and position can buy justice often cite a string of cases from the 1980s and 1990s in which wealthy and prominent defendants won acquittals with the help of the sort of "dream team" criminal lawyers Page referred to. Besides the Simpson case, they include these: Auto manufacturer John DeLorean was acquitted of drug possession and distribution charges, despite an incriminating videotape; his attorneys successfully argued that he had been entrapped by law enforcement agents who set up a "sting" operation by posing as drug traffickers. Imelda Marcos, wife of former Philippines dictator Ferdinand Marcos, was acquitted of stealing $222 million from the Philippines and investing it in New York City real estate. William Kennedy Smith, nephew of U.S. Senator Edward Kennedy, was acquitted of raping a woman at the Kennedy compound in Palm Beach, Florida. And wealthy socialite Claus von Bulow was acquitted on charges that he had put his wife into a permanent coma by injecting her with insulin.

In each of these cases, a jury found in the defendant's favor. The jury members heard and reviewed the evidence, and there's little point in trying to second-guess their findings. Nevertheless, the verdicts were controversial. Many people have questioned whether defendants with less money and little standing would have won acquittal in the same set of circumstances.

In fact, during the same time period, several highly publicized cases resulted in convictions for people who were poor or had only average means: Pamela Smart, a high-school aide in New Hampshire, was found guilty of seducing a fifteen-year-old student and convincing him

Some people believed that William Kennedy Smith's acquittal in a high-profile 1991 rape case supported the belief that money can buy justice.

Susan Smith was a single mother of limited means who was convicted of killing her two young sons. If she had had access to higher-caliber legal representation, would the results have been different?

and his friends to murder her husband. She was sentenced to life in prison. Yolanda Saldivar was convicted of deliberately killing the popular Tejano singer Selena, for whom she managed a boutique; a jury rejected her statement that the shooting was an accident. Five teenage members of a Houston, Texas, gang were sentenced to die by lethal injection after they were convicted of raping and strangling two teenage girls who happened to come across the gang during an initiation ceremony. A South Carolina mother, Susan Smith, was found guilty of drowning her two children, aged fourteen months and three years, by strapping them into safety seats and rolling her car into a lake. Francisco Martin Duran, a Colorado upholsterer, received a forty-year prison sentence for trying to shoot President Bill Clinton. Duran had fired at the White House; no one was hurt.

The question that is raised about these cases is not so much whether the verdicts were just as whether money might have made a difference in the outcome.

Money Matters. Just what is it that money buys in court? First, it buys top-flight trial lawyers, many of whom command fees of up to $400 an hour. When pretrial proceedings and the trial itself drag on for months, attorneys' bills easily reach hundreds of thousands of dollars. Simpson's defense team included some of the top legal names in the country. Johnnie Cochran, who led the team, was backed up by F. Lee Bailey, Carl Douglas, Robert Shapiro, Alan Dershowitz, Barry Scheck, and three other well-known attorneys—more lawyers than had ever joined together to defend a single person in U.S. legal history. There's little doubt that Simpson's defense also produced some of the largest legal bills in U.S. history.

Of course, having fame and connections doesn't hurt, either. Celebrities and other public figures who have a good public image may find that this works to their advantage with a jury—people are predisposed to like them. And high-profile cases involving prominent people often attract high-profile attorneys, who know that the intense publicity that surrounds such cases is bound to enhance their reputations.

Money also makes it possible to hire jury consultants and conduct the kind of opinion research described in Chapter 2. The consultants can draw up psychological

O. J. Simpson's "Dream Team" of lawyers, including (from left to right) Carl Douglas, Johnnie Cochran, and Robert Shapiro, succeeded in doing what they were paid dearly to do: obtain an acquittal for their client.

profiles of potentially sympathetic jurors and help ensure that the jury will be at least open, and at best favorably inclined, to their client's case. And opinion research allows the lawyers to shape their arguments to appeal to the jurors.

With money, a legal team can afford to fly in experts from around the country and have them testify at the trial, and to hire a lab to run its own tests on physical evidence. In a criminal case, by presenting experts and analyses that contradict the prosecution's witnesses, the defense increases its chances of undermining the prosecution's case and raising questions in the minds of the jurors. That may be all that's needed for acquittal, under the standard of proof required in criminal cases. As one observer put it, "Money buys reasonable doubt."[3]

Is the situation so different for defendants who aren't wealthy? Most people who stand accused of crimes think it well worthwhile to hire a good trial lawyer, but few can afford a "dream team" legal defense with all the bells and whistles. What about poor defendants who cannot afford a lawyer at all? They still have a constitutional right to legal representation, but until the 1960s that didn't mean they would get it. Courts asked local attorneys to volunteer their time to represent poor defendants pro bono (from the Latin *pro bono publico*, "for the public good"), as part of the lawyers' duty to society. But this generally was done only in capital cases, where the death penalty was at stake, or in cases where the defendant was judged mentally backward. Someone accused of a simple offense, such as breaking and entering, might have no representation at all.

That changed with the Supreme Court ruling in the case of *Gideon* v. *Wainwright* in 1963. Clarence Earl Gideon was charged with breaking into a Panama City,

Clarence Earl Gideon (right) fought for his constitutional right for legal counsel and won. After his release from prison in 1963, he spoke on the radio with talk-show host Larry King.

Florida, poolroom, where he stole a pint of wine and some coins from a cigarette machine. The trial court refused to appoint a lawyer for him, and he couldn't afford one. He was convicted. From prison, he wrote his own petition (in pencil), and the Supreme Court ruled in his favor. He won a new trial, with an attorney this time, and was acquitted.

Because of the ruling, poor defendants like him were guaranteed the right to legal representation in serious criminal cases. Justice Hugo L. Black wrote: "The right of one charged with crime to counsel may not be deemed fundamental and essential in some countries, but it is in ours."[4]

Today a defendant in a criminal case who can't afford representation is assigned a court-appointed lawyer, or public defender. That still may leave the poor defendant at a disadvantage, however. A court-appointed lawyer may or may not represent a poor defendant well. Few lawyers rush to take this work, which in some states pays as little as $20 an hour. Many public defenders are dedicated, skilled professionals. Most are overworked, and some are disinterested or incompetent. The defendant has to take the luck of the draw. A private organization, the Legal Aid Society, may help poor defendants, but its resources are strained by the sheer volume of cases.

If the prosecution's case is weak and the defense case is strong, all this may not matter. The jury that hears clear evidence is likely to come to a reasonable verdict. It's when the evidence is unclear, or heavily against the defendant, that a high-ticket defense team may make the difference. Ordinary people are likely to plea-bargain, pleading guilty to reduced charges to avoid a trial with an uncertain outcome. Those who can afford a top defense attorney will get someone like Alan Dershowitz, who represented Claus von Bulow and other high-profile defendants, as well as O. J. Simpson. Dershowitz once wrote: "Almost all criminal defendants—including most of my clients—are guilty of the crimes they have been charged with. The criminal lawyer's job, for the most part, is to represent the guilty, and—if possible—to get them off."[5]

At the other end of the scale is the case of Cornelius Singleton, a black man who was tried, convicted, and executed in 1992 for the bizarre crime of killing a nun in a cemetery by smothering her with rocks. One writer gave this account of the trial: "After begging to be taken off the case, the court-appointed lawyer refused to meet with his client, failed to object when the prosecutor struck all blacks from the jury pool, and neglected to tell the jury that Singleton was mentally retarded. He then forged Singleton's name on a petition for habeas corpus; he was later disbarred."[6] With such representation to rely on, it's not surprising that many poor defendants take whatever deal the prosecution offers.

When it comes to civil cases, the high legal costs and other expenses associated with lawsuits are out of the reach of average people. In fact, most people who think about bringing a lawsuit drop the idea when they learn just how much it is likely to cost. People who are on the receiving end of a suit pray their insurance will cover the costs. And lawsuits simply aren't a realistic option for poor people, unless they can convince an attorney to take the case pro bono or on contingency, so that the lawyer is paid out of any settlement money won. The federal Legal Services Corporation, set up in 1974 to help in civil cases, has suffered staff and budget cutbacks and handles only the most serious cases.

Is Justice for Sale? No one argues that American courts are corrupt, in the sense that judges or juries can be bribed. But it would be difficult to conclude that wealth and fame are not advantages in court, and many people find that deeply troubling. If a trial were a sports event, in which defense and prosecuting attorneys were competing for a prize awarded by the jury, no one would find it strange that some players are better equipped than others. But the goal is justice—fair and evenhanded enforcement of the law. When the system falls short of the ideal, people lose faith in it.

Supreme Court justice Hugo Black wrote that, under the Constitution, the American legal system requires "equal justice for poor and rich, weak and powerful alike," and that there "can be no equal justice where the kind of trial a man gets depends on the amount of money he has." But money, argues Harvard University law professor Richard Parker, is "precisely what the 'kind of trial a man gets' still depends on."[7]

Parker is among the legal scholars who find both injustice and enormous waste in the current trial system. He sees two paths to reform. The first would be to greatly increase lawyers' responsibilities to take court-assigned cases, or to take cases at reduced fees. This doesn't seem likely to happen—in fact, with governments under budget pressure, there are proposals to reduce or eliminate government-subsidized legal aid for the poor.

A second option might be to lessen the roles of defense and prosecuting attorneys, so that a trial would be less a battle between adversaries than a review of the evidence. For example, judges would be required to "sift, assemble, and present most evidence to juries and to sharply restrict the extravagance of lawyers on both sides."[8] Trials would be much shorter—and it would be much harder to manipulate the jury. But such major changes in the court system won't be made quickly.

Chapter Five
Trial by Television

*The authors of the Bill of Rights did not undertake
to assign priorities between First Amendment and
Sixth Amendment rights, ranking one as superior
to the other.*[1]

—Chief Justice Warren E. Burger

In June 1994, millions of Americans watched on television as police cruisers stalked O. J. Simpson's white Ford Bronco down Los Angeles freeways. Network news teams interrupted programming to give live coverage to the slow-speed car chase. And that was just the start of the extraordinary publicity that surrounded the Simpson case. From arrest to acquittal, the news media gave it saturation coverage. The cable network Court TV provided live coverage of the trial itself. The major networks reported on events in the courtroom several times daily, while Cable News Network (CNN) offered longer reports and talk-show commentary from legal experts. Before the trial was fully under way, one poll reported that as many as 84 percent of Americans were fed up with the amount of coverage given the case. And yet they continued to watch . . . and watch, and watch. In April 1995, another poll showed that 40 million Americans, about a fourth of all adults, were tuning in to all or most of the trial coverage.[2]

At about the same time, a case that caused nearly equal public fascination was coming to trial in Toronto, Canada. There, a man named Paul Bernardo stood accused of murdering two young women. His former wife, Karla Homolka, had already been convicted of manslaughter for her role in the killings, and she was serving a twelve-year sentence. Canadians had been following the case for two years, but they still knew relatively little about the details. News coverage was tightly restricted, and even the details of Karla Homolka's 1993 trial were off-limits to reporters. Television cameras were banned from the courthouse. TV crews set up across the street, but they could report the trial's progress only indirectly. "In the Simpson case, the press has been allowed to print all kinds of things, and TV coverage has been excessive," sniffed a Canadian defense attorney. "We simply don't allow that kind of circus."[3]

Because Canadian courts strictly limit news coverage of criminal cases, it was easier to find potential jurors who had not already formed opinions about Bernardo's guilt or innocence, and there was little need to worry about how press coverage might affect the jury during the trial. But limiting news coverage left the public with unanswered questions. When details of Homolka's trial weren't released, people began to wonder: Had she been given a fair trial? Did prosecutors go easy with her in exchange for testimony against Bernardo? Restricted news coverage also contributed to doubts about the criminal justice system in general. "People have questions about how the whole process works. It seems very mysterious and abstract to most people in our society, a world unto itself," an official with the Canadian Bar Association observed.[4]

The contrast between the California and Canadian trials points up two very different views of the role of the media in court proceedings. Americans have a long history of openness where court cases are concerned, while Canada follows the British legal system in restricting what can be broadcast and published. There are arguments for, and against, each view.

A Public Trial. The founders of the United States saw the constitutional guarantee of a "public trial" as a way of ensuring judicial fairness. They knew that when court proceedings are carried on in secret, the potential for bias and unfairness is far higher than it is when members of the public are free to watch. Witnesses are more likely to speak the truth, and judges and prosecutors are more likely to act fairly, when the public is watching. And people are more likely to have faith in the justice system when they can observe its workings. In a sense, when reporters cover a trial, they're acting as representatives of all the people who can't actually attend. The media's right to report open court proceedings also enjoys the protection of the First Amendment, which guarantees freedom of the press.

Open trials and freedom of the press are core values of a democratic society. However, these rights sometimes conflict with another constitutional guarantee: the right to trial by an impartial jury. The concern that extensive coverage of a case before or during a trial may bias jurors goes back to the early days of the American judicial system. In 1807, Chief Justice of the Supreme Court John Marshall faced the problem in the treason trial of Aaron Burr. Few people in the area of Virginia that provided the jury pool hadn't read about the case in newspapers, discussed it with their neighbors, or formed some opinion about Burr, who had served as vice president. After lengthy questioning, Marshall finally seated the jurors needed. He also established a basic standard: Jurors couldn't be considered impartial if they were so influenced by what they saw and read outside the courtroom that they couldn't base a decision solely on evidence presented in court.

The voir dire process is supposed to uncover such bias, but it's often difficult to know just how much influence media coverage has had. Once a jury is impaneled, the jurors can be instructed not to read or watch news reports about a case; but in a high-profile case such news can be hard to avoid. The greatest risk is that the jurors will see media reports of matters that would be considered inadmissible in court: information about a defendant's criminal record, an involuntary (coerced) confession, evidence that was obtained through illegal means (such as a search conducted without a warrant). This material may be damning, but it's excluded to keep law enforcement authorities from abusing their powers.

News reports can influence public opinion, too. Sensational coverage that dwells on the brutal aspects of a crime can rouse anger against a defendant. On the other hand, coverage can glorify criminals and give them heroic status—portraying fugitives and gangsters, for example, as romantic or glamorous figures.

How can courts ensure that media coverage won't influence the jury? The most direct ways are to bar news crews and the rest of the public from court proceedings, seal documents relating to a case, or even prohibit press reports about a case. That's the position taken by British courts, which sharply limit the press accounts in criminal cases. One British newspaper was even cited for contempt of court for referring to a "murder" before a trial had firmly established that the killing was, in fact, murder.

In the United States, however, reporters have challenged attempts to restrict their access to court proceedings—with some success. In a 1979 ruling, the Supreme Court gave judges wide leeway to close courtrooms during pretrial proceedings, finding a "constitutional duty to minimize the effects of prejudicial pretrial publicity."[5] (Pretrial hearings determine, among other things, what evidence will be admissible in the actual trial. The press unsuccessfully argued that, since so many cases end in plea bargaining at this stage, news coverage was essential.)

But that leeway doesn't extend to trials. In other cases, the Court has held that a judge must have very strong reasons indeed for closing a trial to the public. Even a defendant's wish to waive the right to a public trial and bar the press from court isn't, in itself, enough to justify the decision. "The right to a fair trial by a jury of one's peers is unquestionably one of the most precious and sacred safeguards enshrined," wrote former Supreme Court Justice William Brennan in one opinion. "I would hold, however, that to resort to prior restraints on the freedom of the press is a constitutionally impermissible method for enforcing that right; judges have at their disposal a broad spectrum of devices for ensuring that fundamental fairness is accorded the accused."[6]

Ensuring Fairness. What are the "devices" that Brennan referred to? Once a trial begins, a judge can order the jury to be sequestered, to shield members from press reports. But even before jurors are chosen, courts can take several steps to make sure that inappropriate news coverage won't affect the case.

One option is to change the venue, or location, for a trial. Venues are often changed when particularly shocking or brutal crimes capture the attention of the communities where they were committed, making it likely that people there will have opinions and strong feelings about them. The federal government took this step in the trial of Timothy McVeigh and Terry Nichols, accused of the terrorist bombing of a federal office building in Oklahoma City, Oklahoma, in 1995. Because many of the 168 people killed in the bombing lived in Oklahoma City, Oklahomans were deeply affected by the crime. The trial was moved to Denver, Colorado, to improve the chance of seating jurors who hadn't already formed an opinion on the case.

Gag orders are another tool for limiting publicity. A court may not be able to prevent the media from reporting information they obtain, but it can order people involved in the case not to discuss it with reporters. Gag orders are commonly used to avoid tainting a jury pool with pretrial publicity, but they don't always work to the advantage of the defendant. For example, before the rape trial of William Kennedy Smith, prosecutors filed papers with the court stating that they had evidence that the defendant had previously raped one woman and attempted to rape two others. While such accusations weren't likely to be allowed as evidence in the trial, the filing was a matter of public record, and the media picked up on it and reported the charges. Defense attorneys were furious because a court-imposed gag order prevented them from speaking directly to the media to counter the accusations.

In fact, the legal community is divided on the question of whether an attorney should argue a case in the public forum provided by the media. Bar association ethics rules forbid lawyers from making statements that could prejudice an upcoming trial. But some defense attorneys believe they must work to clear their clients "both in the court of law and the court of public opinion," and they actively seek out the press. Notes one legal scholar: "There is still no solid evidence that pretrial publicity makes it impossible to get jurors to decide a case based on court evidence rather than what's in newspapers or on TV. But defense lawyers are more aware of their need to present their clients' case at the same time the public is exposed to the prosecution's charges."[7]

How Much Is Too Much? Just as views about what's acceptable for defense attorneys have shifted over the years, so have views about what's acceptable in media coverage. In the early 1900s, sensational (and opinionated) crime reporting was a staple newspaper feature. The trend peaked in the 1932 trial of Bruno Richard Hauptmann, charged with kidnapping and killing the infant child of the famous pilot Charles Lindbergh. The fact that Lindbergh was a national hero meant that the case received extraordinary publicity from the start. When the trial opened in Flemington, New Jersey, spectators and reporters packed the courtroom, and an overflow crowd gathered outside the open windows. Photographers and newsreel camera operators were allowed inside, and flashbulbs popped constantly as they recorded the proceedings. The prosecuting and defense attorneys held daily press conferences where they discussed the evidence and offered predictions about the course of the trial. As with the Simpson trial more than sixty years later, public curiosity about the crime and the trial was insatiable—but at the same time, many people were disgusted by the excessive coverage.

Until the O. J. Simpson trial in 1995, no trial in history had garnered the attention of that of Bruno Richard Hauptmann, charged with kidnapping and killing the baby of aviator Charles Lindbergh in the 1930s. That case first suggested the idea of a trial being a "media circus."

After the Lindbergh kidnapping trial, a joint committee formed by the American Bar Association and several newspaper groups came up with guidelines for press coverage of trials. Among other things, the committee recommended that, during a trial, photographs and sound recording should be banned in court; lawyers should be barred from arguing their case to the public through press releases and press conferences or from publicly criticizing the judge or jury; witnesses should be forbidden to discuss the case in interviews or speeches; and there should be no "popular referendum" on the guilt or innocence of a defendant. The group also recommended that the "featuring in vaudeville of jurors or other court officers, either during or after the trial," be forbidden.[8]

These guidelines were largely followed for many years, but most of them have fallen by the wayside. The Simpson case provided plenty of examples, with extensive media coverage that went far beyond the proceedings in the courtroom. Numerous polls showed how Americans would vote if they were on the jury. Simpson, the prosecuting and defense attorneys, and even trial judge Lance Ito became stock fodder for comedians—not in vaudeville but on television. NBC's *Tonight Show With Jay Leno* even featured a spoof called the "Dancing Itos." Some people faulted the media for the excesses, but many felt the blame should be shared. True, the media focused on the colorful personalities involved in the case; but, far from shunning the attention and refusing to discuss the case, the attorneys and witnesses played to the media. That drew attention away from the facts and evidence presented in court and helped create a circus atmosphere. Back in the 1930s, FBI director J. Edgar Hoover said of the Lindbergh kidnapping case: "The press is not to blame.

Cameras in the courtroom brought the O. J. Simpson trial to living rooms all over the country, and undoubtedly contributed to the media frenzy that followed almost every aspect of the case and every personality involved in it.

If you put on a freak show the press will report it as such."[9] Much the same could be said of the Simpson trial.

Cameras in Court. One of the most intense current debates involves the presence of television cameras in court. Bans on courtroom photography began to crumble in the 1950s and 1960s, when better films and cameras allowed pictures to be taken in natural light—so that no flashbulbs interrupted the proceedings. States began to let individual judges decide whether to allow still and, later, television cameras in their courtrooms. Cameras are still not permitted in federal criminal cases, but by 1995 they were common in state courtrooms.

The trend has been praised in some cases, condemned in others. In a courtroom, some people argue, television cameras help create an overheated "celebrity" atmosphere that distracts everyone involved in a case—judge, witnesses, attorneys, jurors. Televised coverage was blamed in part for the deadlock that ended the first trial of Lyle and Erik Menendez, in which two separate juries (one for each defendant) could not reach a verdict on the charge that the brothers had killed their parents. When the brothers were retried, cameras and microphones were barred from the courtroom.

Live coverage was similarly faulted in the Simpson trial. After the trial, however, Judge Lance Ito defended his decision to allow cameras in court. "The American public got to see for themselves every day, all day, how this trial progressed—what the jury saw and what the jury wasn't allowed to see because of some of the rulings I made," Ito said. "The problem with not having a camera is that one must trust the evaluation and analysis of a reporter who's telling you what occurred in the courtroom,

(73)

and anytime you allow somebody to report an event, you have to take into consideration the filtering effect of that person's own biases."[10]

Rikki J. Klieman, a former prosecutor and defense lawyer who covered the Simpson trial for Court TV, also defended the camera's role: "Through years of experience, I learned that jurors and witnesses were no more affected by one camera in the back of the courtroom than they were by one more spectator. The camera simply became part of the landscape." Moreover, she added, "With the camera in the courtroom, we are able to scrutinize the work of elected officials as well as public defenders and superstars of the bar. Public scrutiny is essential, not only for justice, but for the appearance of justice in a system of balanced government. . . . If the camera reveals the flaws as well as the virtues of the system, it becomes a vehicle for observation, reflection, and change—three excellent goals for journalism as well as for justice."[11]

Nevertheless, the trend after the Simpson trial was to limit live coverage in high-profile trials. When relatives of the victims in the Simpson case followed the criminal trial with a civil suit against the former football star, the judge in that case barred all cameras and recorders from the courtroom.

Chapter Six

The Rights of
the Defendant

*Nothing can destroy a government more quickly
than its failure to observe its own laws, or worse,
its disregard of the charter of its own existence.*[1]
—Supreme Court Justice Tom C. Clark

Late one night in the fall of 1990, a rented van whisked
past a New York state police car at 70 miles (110 kilome-
ters) an hour. The troopers gave chase and stopped the
van; then, because hunting season was under way and
they wanted to check for illegal deer carcasses and loaded
rifles, they asked to look in the van's cargo section. The
driver obliged and opened up the back of the van, which
held some construction equipment, a box of clothing, and
a steamer trunk. But when the troopers asked to see what
was in the trunk, the driver suddenly turned tail and ran.
The reason was clear as soon as the troopers opened the
trunk: Inside it was the body of Fernando Cuervo, who
had been shot to death.

    The driver, Leonardo Turriago, was arrested and con-
victed of Cuervo's murder. The evidence against him was

overwhelming, even Turriago's attorneys agreed. Besides the body, the police found the murder weapon (which the killer had tossed into the Hudson River) and drugs and guns in Turriago's New York City apartment. He began serving a prison sentence of forty-five years to life. But in June 1996, Turriago's conviction was overturned on appeal. A state appeals court ruled that the troopers' search of the van was illegal because they had neither a warrant nor "founded suspicion that criminality was afoot"—that is, until they looked in the trunk, they had no reason to think that Turriago had done anything other than exceed the speed limit. Because the body was found in an illegal search, it should not have been used as evidence against him, the court said.[2]

The decision prompted outrage, and some people immediately seized on it as an example of a deplorable trend in which courts have granted so many protections to defendants that criminals like Turriago routinely go free. In fact, the Turriago case was extreme. New York's requirement that police have "founded suspicion" for a warrantless search is unusual. In most states, and in federal courts, the search would have been legal simply because Turriago consented to it. But his is not the only case in which a defendant who seemed clearly guilty went free because the police or the courts failed to follow procedures designed to protect innocent people. The concern that the American legal system has gone too far in protecting defendants is widespread and genuine.

Yet so is the concern that innocent people will be railroaded into jail if law enforcement powers are unchecked. Examples of injustice abound. Just a few weeks after the Turriago conviction was reversed, for example, three Chicago men were finally released after serving eighteen years in prison for a double murder they didn't commit. They were arrested and convicted in 1978. (A fourth man, arrested with them, was initially released but arrested again and convicted in 1984; he had been cleared a few weeks earlier.) "The police just picked up the first four young black men they could, and that was it. They didn't care if we were guilty or innocent," said Dennis Williams, one of the three men. He had spent most of his prison time on Death Row.[3]

How much protection should be given to defendants in criminal cases or to convicted criminals? The New York and Chicago cases touch on two aspects of this question where debate has been especially sharp. One of those aspects is the so-called exclusionary rule, which bars from a jury's consideration evidence that is obtained in violation of the Fourth Amendment's guarantee of "the right of the people to be secure in their persons, houses, papers, and effects, against unreasonable searches and seizures." The second is the appeals process, especially the appeals mounted by convicts on Death Row, which some people feel are allowed to drag on far too long.

Search and Seizure. The Fourth Amendment's ban on "unreasonable" searches and seizures requires the police to go before a judge or magistrate and obtain a warrant that specifically describes the place to be searched and the articles to be seized. For that, the police must show "probable cause" for the action. In effect, before they can proceed, they must convince a court that the action is reasonable—that there is reason to think that evidence of crime will be found.

The authors of the Bill of Rights were keenly aware of the need for this amendment. In the period leading up to the Revolutionary War, King George III of England issued so-called writs of assistance to his agents. The writs gave the agents blanket authority to search for smuggled goods wherever and whenever they wished, and they abused the power so widely that their searches helped fuel the spirit of rebellion. In 1761 the early Revolutionary leader James Otis declared that writs of assistance were "the worst instrument of arbitrary power," because they put "the liberty of every man in the hands of every officer." John Adams, one of the key figures of the period, later wrote of Otis's speech: "Then and there the child of Independence was born."[4]

Until the twentieth century, however, the protection offered by the Fourth Amendment was uneven at best. If police officers chose to knock down a person's door in the middle of the night, and search his or her home cellar to attic without a warrant, the only recourse was to file a lawsuit against the police after the fact. Faced with the prospect of a court battle, legal fees, and a jury's likely sympathy with police, few people did. And since it was especially hard for poor people and members of minority groups to bring suit and win compensation, they were often victims of unjustified searches. They were also most likely to encounter other abuses in the system. For example, it was routine for police to take people into custody for questioning, in a sweeping "dragnet" that brought in vagrants, people with prior convictions, and anyone else who seemed suspicious.

What became known as the exclusionary rule was first set out by the Supreme Court in 1914. In *Weeks* v. *United States*, the Court said that illegally obtained evidence would no longer be accepted in federal courts. The ruling was later extended to state courts, but in some areas it was widely ignored. That began to change in the 1960s, as the Supreme Court and federal appeals courts reviewed and overturned hundreds of convictions from state courts. Among the famous cases was *Mapp* v. *Ohio*, in which the Supreme Court ruled that evidence seized in an unlawful search (in this case, without a warrant) could not be used in a state criminal trial.

Gradually uniform standards emerged covering not only search and seizure but other rights, including the right to counsel and the right to be free from warrantless arrest and unreasonable detention. Courts began to bar evidence of guilt, even confessions, that had been obtained when these rights were violated. In 1966 the Supreme Court overturned the conviction (for kidnapping and rape) of Ernesto Miranda, who had been interrogated for hours by police and had signed a confession without being told that he had a right to remain silent and to have a lawyer present. As a result, police officers were trained to follow procedures that would comply with court rulings and to inform suspects of their "Miranda" rights. Misconduct by the police was sharply curbed.

Reaction to the Exclusionary Rule. Since the 1960s, however, rising crime rates have helped create a reaction against the exclusionary rule. The increase in crime has complex causes, among them growing drug abuse, the flight of jobs and middle-class workers from cities, and the resulting decay of inner-city neighborhoods. These social problems are difficult to fix, and that has tempted many people to search for causes to correct that can be addressed more easily. One is the idea that crime is increasing because courts are bending over backward to defend individual rights and, in the process, allowing criminals to go free on "legal technicalities." Some observers blame as much as 15 percent of the increase in crime on the exclusionary rule, saying that it frees at least 20,000 criminals a year.[5]

But supporters of the exclusionary rule cite different statistics. Studies by the U.S. General Accounting Office, the American Bar Association, and other groups indicate that only 1 to 2 percent of criminal cases are dismissed because of the rule.[6] Moreover, courts allow warrantless searches and seizures in a wide range of exceptions— when evidence is sitting in plain view, when the police are in hot pursuit of a suspected criminal, when evidence may be destroyed if the police wait to get a warrant, or even when police err in good faith (acting on a warrant that later turns out to have expired, for example). A 1988 ABA study showed that most police "do not consider search and seizure proscriptions to be a serious obstacle."[7]

Should the exclusionary rule be curtailed or perhaps thrown out altogether? A bill introduced in Congress in 1995 would have done just that by allowing any law enforcement officer to conduct a warrantless search on the "objectively reasonable belief" that the action wouldn't violate the Fourth Amendment. Supporters of the bill argued that police regulations were enough to limit abuse, and that anyone who felt victimized by a search could sue for damages. (The bill would have limited the amount that could be awarded, however.) Opponents said that by transferring the authority to approve searches from courts to individual police officers, the bill would have been a return to the days of colonial writs of assistance. And in the past, lawsuits and police regulations weren't enough to ensure fairness; that was why the Supreme Court came up with the rule in the first place.

Even supporters of the exclusionary rule agree that it has flaws, especially when it leads to the release of a violent criminal. Yet most Americans (nearly 70 percent, in one poll) are uncomfortable with the idea of warrantless searches like those in the 1995 bill, which passed the House of Representatives but not the Senate.[8] With lawmakers staking out firm political positions on each side of the issue, debate seems certain to continue.

Habeas Corpus and Death Row Appeals. The legal action known as habeas corpus evolved over centuries in Great Britain. In the simplest sense, it's a way of protecting citizens from unjust imprisonment. A writ of habeas corpus requires law enforcement authorities to show the legal grounds for holding a person in custody. In the United States today, habeas corpus is mainly used in three situations: to force the police to release a prisoner when no charges have been filed against that person; to make sure that, if charges have been filed, the prisoner has a chance to post bail (unless a judge denies bail); and to ensure that the rights of a person convicted of a crime have not been violated. The third situation is the most common, and it's the one that has given rise to the most controversy.

Long after a defendant has exhausted the usual avenues of appeal, he can file a habeas corpus petition asserting that his rights were violated and asking for a review of the case. State courts receive many such petitions. So do federal courts, when Fourth Amendment or other constitutional guarantees are involved. Under law, federal courts can step in and review state court proceedings, even hold new hearings, and overturn state court decisions in these cases. The Constitution states: "The Privilege of the Writ of Habeas Corpus shall not be suspended, unless when in Cases of Rebellion or Invasion the public safety may require it." And government has rarely tried to limit this right, allowing prisoners to file petitions at any point.

(81)

(Abraham Lincoln suspended it during the Civil War, judging that to be a case of rebellion.) When Japanese Americans were placed in detention camps during World War II, a writ of habeas corpus finally freed them.

In the 1990s, however, there were new calls for limits. The cases of Death Row prisoners who managed to stave off execution for as much as twenty years with a series of appeals drew public attention to the issue. An American Bar Association study showed that as many as 40 percent of these petitions were ultimately granted (showing that they had some basis in law), but critics of the court system argued that the appeals were simply an endless delaying tactic.[9]

As a result of the debate, court rulings and a federal law effectively limited state prison inmates to one habeas corpus petition in federal court. While inmates might still be freed if new evidence turned up proving their innocence, they would have only one chance to appeal the constitutionality of their convictions. The law was immediately challenged as a violation of the Constitution, but in 1996 the Supreme Court upheld it. In other decisions, the Court has also made it more difficult for inmates to win appeals on constitutional grounds. For example, when constitutional errors were found in the past, convictions might be overturned unless the state could show that the errors were harmless. Under new Supreme Court guidelines, federal judges can't throw out a conviction unless the defendant proves the errors had a substantial effect on the jury's verdict.

These changes have drawn support for several reasons. One is concern about crime, a worry that crosses political lines. Even in prison, some people feel, violent criminals are a danger to society—a murderer might escape, or attack a prison guard, or even be released on parole. Those who have been sentenced to die should be executed promptly, they argue, not only to protect society but to carry through the punishment and to spare taxpayers the cost of housing and caring for prisoners. Many political conservatives have supported limits on habeas corpus not only for these reasons but also because of the way these appeals allowed federal courts to control state courts. Limiting habeas corpus is a way to limit federal power over the states.

But there is also strong opposition to placing limits on the appeals process. Opponents are concerned that the new restrictions may make a key constitutional right meaningless. The privilege of habeas corpus has never been limited in this way, they argue: "Since the seventeenth century, courts have said that the right of freedom from illegal restraint never lapses."[10] Moreover, limiting Death Row appeals is bound to lead to errors in which people who might have been freed are executed, opponents say. If the new restrictions had been in place, Dennis Williams and the others freed with him might never have survived eighteen years in prison to be released in 1996, for example. The evidence that finally cleared them took years to come to light.

This argument is tied to a broader debate on the death penalty itself. Opponents of the death penalty believe that the risk of executing innocent people far outweighs any social benefit of this punishment, and they point out that the United States is among the few Western countries that still imposes it. To supporters of the death penalty, errors are an acceptable price. "Innocent people have been executed," says Laurin A. Wollan, Jr., of Florida State University. "The value of the death penalty is its rightness vis-à-vis the wrongness of the crime, and that is so valuable that the possibility of the conviction of the innocent, though rare, has to be accepted."[11] But with new rules limiting appeals, opponents worry, the errors may not be so rare. The length of the appeals process may be "well below the average time it takes to discover new evidence," according to Richard C. Dieter, director of the Death Penalty Information Center. "This rush to get on with the death penalty by shortening the appeals process will raise the danger of executing innocent people."[12]

Chapter
Seven
The Rights
of the Victim

*Of all the various kinds of punishment we can in-
flict on any one offender, the one they most de-
serve is the rage of the victims they have hurt.*[1]
   —John Stein, victims' rights advocate

After their nineteen-year-old daughter was killed by her
boyfriend in May 1994, Sam and Wanda Rieger began
an ordeal that left them convinced that American justice
was deeply flawed. "The legal system's efforts are con-
centrated on protecting the criminal's rights, not the rights
of the victim," Sam Rieger, a professor of chemistry at a
Connecticut college, told a local newspaper. "Our daughter was murdered, and we have to go through a brutal
court system that denies the victim any part in the court
proceedings. It is the state versus the criminal. And you
are told you can sit in the courtroom but you can't show
any emotion. You're not allowed to become angry or upset by anything that goes on. You can't even cry."[2]
   Indeed, after his daughter's killer won a postpone-
ment of his trial by claiming that he had a multiple per-

sonality disorder and needed psychiatric evaluation, Rieger was reprimanded by the judge for slamming the door on the way out of the courtroom. Further postponements delayed the trial until January 1996, when the killer was convicted. Meanwhile, Rieger had taken action to solve the problems he saw in the justice system. He founded a local chapter of Parents of Murdered Children and Other Survivors of Homicide Victims, a group that promotes better treatment for victims of crime.

Survivors is one of several groups leading a fight for victims' rights. These groups hope to educate law enforcement officials and the public to the enormous pain that crime victims and their families endure—pain that's often made worse by insensitive officials and media publicity. But their goals go beyond winning greater compassion and more sensitive treatment. They want greater involvement in criminal proceedings and a voice in court. Support for victims' rights has grown even as some experts warn that granting such rights may compromise the constitutional guarantee of a fair and impartial trial.

Shoved Aside. Crime victims' perception that they are shoved aside by courts is rooted in the nature of criminal law. A person who robs another at gunpoint commits a crime not only against that individual but against society as a whole. And it's society—in the form of the police, the courts, and prisons—that deals with the criminal. This puts greater resources on the side of law enforcement, avoids the danger of vigilantes roaming the streets in search of their personal version of justice, and ensures that the accused get a fair hearing.

In theory, society's interests and the victim's interests are the same: Catch and punish the criminal. In practice, that's not always the case. A robbery victim may hope to see the robber handed the maximum sentence, but a prosecutor may prefer a plea bargain. Perhaps the case isn't strong, or the prosecutor wants to save the time and cost of a trial. Or perhaps the robber has information about another criminal case and will cooperate with authorities in exchange for lenient treatment. A deal is in society's best interests in such cases. The victim may not see it that way; but because a criminal proceeding is a matter between society and the accused, the victim's role is often limited to giving a statement or appearing as a witness. In murder cases, there may be almost no role for the family and other survivors of the victim. As Sam Rieger described it, "You just sit there and can't say anything. It's a helpless feeling."[3] When victims or survivors are to testify at a trial, they often aren't even allowed to watch the proceedings—because the evidence presented, and the testimony of other witnesses, might lead them to alter their testimony.

Victims and survivors who feel cheated by the outcome of a trial have few options. One is to file a civil lawsuit against the defendant. After the Simpson murder trial ended in acquittal, for example, the families of Nicole Brown Simpson and Ron Goldman filed suit against O. J. Simpson in civil court, claiming damages on the grounds that he had caused the "wrongful death" of the victims. With a new judge and jury, much of the same evidence was presented—but this time, the courtroom was closed to cameras, and there was far less publicity. There was also a different standard of proof. While the prosecution in a criminal case must prove the defendant guilty "beyond a reasonable doubt," the prosecution in a civil case need only show that a "preponderance of the evidence"

The family of Ronald Goldman has spoken out for victims'
rights, and pursued the ultimate right of a victim's
survivors: filing suit against the accused in civil court,
claiming damages for "wrongful death."

(that is, more than half the weight of the evidence) indicates guilt.

Most crime victims don't pursue lawsuits, however. One major reason is that most criminals aren't wealthy and won't be able to pay damage awards in any event. Some states have victim compensation statutes, mandating that criminals make payments to victims. But for the same reason, these laws often don't provide much relief. Some legal scholars have proposed another option: Let crime victims sue the government, which, they argue, is charged with protecting citizens from crime. This is a concept that has a long history in English law. In fact, before World War II many states had "riot laws," requiring them to compensate citizens whose property was damaged in riots and other civil disturbances that the government was supposed to prevent. But these laws are no longer on the books. And meanwhile, victims have grown increasingly angry with the system. Since the 1960s, their frustration has increased in step with the push to enforce defendants' rights through measures such as the exclusionary rule.

Victims' Rights. The victims' rights movement began to gather steam in the 1970s, as crime (and the tendency of prosecutors to offer plea bargains as a way to speed cases through court) increased. The National Organization for Victim Assistance (NOVA), founded in 1975, and other groups were formed to change the way crime victims are treated. Among the guarantees they have proposed are these:

• Victims should have a right to be informed of, be present at, and be heard at every important stage of a criminal case. Some advocates believe victims should be consulted before prosecutors agree to plea-bargain with defendants, for example.

(89)

• Just as the Sixth Amendment guarantees a defendant the right to a speedy trial, the victim of a crime should have the right to see the case brought to trial quickly, without procedural delays that would drag it out for years.

• Victims should have the right to present statements in court (if not during the trial itself; then, if the defendant is convicted, before sentencing), to tell the judge (or jury) about the impact of the crime. The purpose, according to NOVA deputy director John Stein, is "not to influence the judge" but "to express hatred for what [the defendant] had done." Confronting the criminal directly in court allows victims a measure of personal satisfaction. Advocates see it as a balance to the defendant's constitutional right to confront prosecution witnesses.[4]

In 1982 a presidential task force on crime victims backed many of these proposals. And since then, many states have adopted at least some of them. Most states now provide some mechanism through which victims are kept informed and are consulted as a criminal case winds its way through the legal system. About twenty states guarantee some form of victims' rights in their constitutions. Most states also permit statements about the impact of a crime to be submitted to the court before sentencing. However, the statements generally aren't made by the victims—they're written by an official who considers the suffering of the victims and tries to make an impartial judgment about the effect of the crime. Only a few states, among them New York and California, permit crime victims to speak personally in court.

The Debate. Victims' statements can be dramatic and moving. Such was the case at the sentencing of Colin Ferguson, convicted of killing six people in a three-minute shooting rampage on a Long Island commuter train in 1993. Fifteen people, including relatives of the murder

A survivor of the Long Island Rail Road shootings in 1993 testifies at the trial of Colin Ferguson, who confessed to the crimes. The emotional accounts of the survivors and the victims' families were a factor in the judge's decision to sentence Ferguson to two hundred years in prison.

victims and others who were shot but survived, took the stand in the New York courtroom. One of the survivors, a building contractor who had been shot in the chest, called the defendant an "animal" and said that if he had five minutes alone with him, "this coward would know the meaning of suffering."[5] Several asked for the maximum sentence, and one asked for the death penalty, which was not available in New York at that time. They welcomed the chance to speak. "The pain in our lives has not changed dramatically, but I felt really good" after testifying, said a woman whose husband and son were both shot on the train. "I had a much lighter heart."[6] The victims and survivors burst into applause when, saying he had been moved by their anger, the judge sentenced Ferguson to two hundred years in prison.

Prosecutors in particular have welcomed the wider use of impact statements. Said one, "The criminal justice system has evolved to the point where it is not just adjudicating the guilt or innocence of the defendant but is really more of a social response to a crime that necessarily includes a victim's family."[7] Many legal experts find the use of victim-impact statements disturbing, however. An editorial in *The New Republic* set out this view:

> *Yelling epithets in a courtroom may indeed be therapeutic for victims, but personal therapy is not a defensible purpose of criminal trials, which are conducted in the name of the people at large. . . . The most basic requirement of the rule of law is that judges and juries must be personally impartial, that they can't decide even close cases on the basis of their sympathy or distaste for one party or another. Yet victim im-*

*pact statements, when presented orally without
the possibility of rational evaluation, guarantee that trials will degenerate into lawless emo-
tionalism.*[8]

The argument is sharpened when the death penalty is at
stake. For many years Supreme Court rulings barred impact statements in capital cases. The justices reasoned that
such factors as the character of the victim and the suffering of the victim's family had nothing to do with the basic
questions of the defendant's actions and intentions, and
thus shouldn't color the decision on whether to condemn
him to death. Punishment, as one legal scholar described
this view, "ought to turn on the reprehensibility of the
criminal and his prior record. The persuasiveness of the
victim's surviving relatives should have nothing to do with
the sentence."[9] Then, in a 1991 case, the Court said that
judges could take impact statements into account in cases
where the death penalty was a possibility, as long as the
statements dealt only with the harm done by the crime
and were free of emotional opinions about what fate the
defendant deserved. But as the statements in the Ferguson
case show, it can be hard to keep emotion out when a
murder victim's survivors speak directly to the court.

Laws granting new rights to victims and survivors are
still being challenged, generally on the grounds that they
interfere with the defendant's right to a fair trial. In New
Jersey, where a state law was adopted permitting survivors to make court statements in capital cases, a superior
court judge found that the law violated the state constitution. "The emotionally powerful nature of victim-impact
evidence is unmistakable," he said.[10] In Utah, a man convicted of rape appealed on the grounds that the victim

had been allowed to watch the entire trial, and thus had a chance to tailor her testimony to agree with that of other witnesses. In Texas, a law that allowed parole boards to consult privately with victims was thrown out because it gave prisoners no way to answer the statements that victims made to the board. There are questions about other rights that victims want, too. For example, if victims are granted the right to a speedy trial, will cases go to trial before the defense has enough time to gather evidence and build its case? That, too, would be a violation of the defendant's right to due process, opponents say.

Nothing in the U.S. Constitution grants rights to crime victims, but that may change. In 1996 both major political parties endorsed the idea of amending the Constitution to include rights for victims. The questions of how far those rights should extend, and how they can be balanced with the Constitution's long-standing protections for people accused of crimes, continue to be debated.

Chapter
Eight
The Trial
Game

Where law ends, tyranny begins.[1]
—William Pitt

For all its flaws, the American legal system is still far superior to the systems in place in many parts of the world. There are many countries where courts are corrupt or under the sway of the government, and where people have no guarantee of a fair trial. But it would be a mistake to conclude that, because other countries have such severe problems, the problems in the American system aren't serious and don't need to be addressed. A few instances of injustice—or even the appearance of injustice—are all that are needed to undermine confidence in the system.

Many of the problems covered in this book stem from competing rights: the First Amendment's guarantee of press freedom versus the Sixth Amendment's guarantee of due process, the rights of defendants versus the rights of victims. The questions these problems raise have been debated almost from the country's founding, and the debate will likely continue for years to come. Other problems are rooted at least in part in the nature of the American court system, in which prosecution and defense are adversaries. The writer Norman Mailer notes: "We don't care to recognize that not only in criminal cases, but even more in civil cases, a trial remains a game. Sometimes it's played for low stakes, sometimes for very high stakes, sometimes by mediocre players, occasionally by extraordinarily skillful players; but even at its best, the most we can say for the process of law in the courts is that it is a game where even justice may occasionally be served."[2]

The adversary system sets up a competition in which wealth (or lack of it) can make or break the ability of an accused person to mount a defense. When the goal is to win, either side may feel justified in trying to impanel the friendliest jury possible, presenting that jury with a skewed version of the facts, or turning to the media to get public opinion on its side. People who think that O. J. Simpson was guilty, writes Richard Parker, will look to see how his lawyers got him off. "They may conclude that his lawyers, his 'officers of the court,' having been delegated power by the adversary system, intentionally used that power to obscure the truth, to derail enforcement of the criminal law . . . . What will most offend them, however, is the disdain for ordinary people revealed as inherent in the adversary system: for the victims and their loved ones, for the people who 'work hard and play by the rules,' and for those who are charged with crimes but who don't have millions of dollars."[3]

The "adversary" aspects of court cases could be reduced with proposals like those outlined in Chapter 4—expanding legal-aid services to put the players on equal footing, and "downsizing" the system by shortening trials and allowing judges to filter and present most of the evidence. But these are major steps and won't come quickly, if ever. More likely are small reforms, such as doing away with jury sequestration, to smooth out some of the kinks in the system. These steps won't lessen the adversary atmosphere of trials, but they may help ensure that responsible juries can reach rational verdicts.

Some of the problems addressed in this book aren't confined to courts; they're reflections of broad social problems, such as racial tensions. If a trial is a game, says Mailer, "From the black point of view, it's a shell game. The whites are holding the pea."[4] The wildly differing views of the justice system held by blacks and whites, some observers argue, are signs that American society is deeply divided. And that, writes Jacob Weisberg, is a bad sign for the country's future: "We simply cannot ratify the notion that there is a white reality and a black reality. A nation that lives with separate realities is Bosnia, not America."[5] Other observers aren't convinced that the situation is quite that serious. Nevertheless, no reform of the court system alone is likely to correct social divisions based on race or on wealth.

Complicating all these issues is the fact that courts today are overwhelmed with civil and criminal cases. Increases in crime and tightening budgets have helped to create a backlog that puts pressure on judges and attorneys to process cases as quickly as possible. There's little time for drawing up and implementing reforms. Still, no matter how difficult it may be, Americans must take steps to correct these problems and ensure that the goal of the trial "game" is justice, not simply victory, and that "players" have an even chance. When people in a segment of society feel that the justice system excludes them, they begin to disrespect and disregard the law—in extreme cases, as criminals or as vigilantes who enforce their own brand of justice.

Notes

Chapter 2

1. Stephen J. Adler, *The Jury: Trial and Error in the American Courtroom* (New York: Random House, 1994), p. 221.
2. Michael Lind, "The Institution from the Dark Ages: Jury Dismissed," *The New Republic*, October 23, 1995.
3. Peter Hunter Blair, *An Introduction to Anglo-Saxon England* (London: Cambridge University Press, 1962), p. 230.
4. Adler, p. 246.
5. Adler, p. 243.
6. Cited by Jeffrey Abramson, *We, the Jury: The Jury System and the Ideal of Democracy* (New York: Basic Books, 1994), p. 45.
7. Sandra Stencel, ed., "The Jury System," *CQ Researcher*, November 10, 1995, p. 998.
8. Stencel, p. 1005.
9. Jan Crawford Greenburg, "The Jury System Goes Under the Microscope," *Chicago Tribune*, October 8, 1995.
10. Adler, p. 113.
11. Adler, p. 43.
12. Adler, p. 239.
13. Abramson, p. 251.
14. Lind.

15. Adler, p. 242.
16. Greenburg.

Chapter 3

1. *Facts on File*, October 5, 1995, p. 727.
2. Fox Butterfield, "Study Finds a Disparity in Justice for African Americans," *The New York Times*, February 13, 1996.
3. Linda Greenhouse, "Race Statistics Alone Do Not Support a Claim of Selective-Prosecution, Justices Rule," *The New York Times*, May 14, 1996.
4. Survey by the Center on Juvenile and Criminal Justice, San Francisco, reported in Butterfield, "Study Finds a Disparity."
5. Butterfield.
6. Sandra Stencel, ed., "The Jury System," *CQ Researcher*, November 10, 1995, p. 1002.
7. Jan Crawford Greenburg, "The Jury System Goes Under the Microscope," *Chicago Tribune*, October 8, 1995.
8. Michael Lind, "The Institution from the Dark Ages: Jury Dismissed," *The New Republic*, October 23, 1995.
9. Stencel, p. 997.
10. Paul Butler, "Racially Based Jury Nullification: Black Power in the Criminal Justice System," *Yale Law Journal*, December 1995.
11. Jacob Weisberg, "The Truth Card," *New York*, October 16, 1995, p. 33.
12. Greenburg, "The Jury System Goes Under the Microscope."
13. Clarence Page, "When Race and Justice Collide," *Chicago Tribune*, October 8, 1995.

Chapter 4

1. Quoted in Milton Meltzer, *The Bill of Rights: How We Got It and What It Means* (New York: Crowell, 1990), p. 141.

2. Clarence Page, "When Race and Justice Collide," *Chicago Tribune*, October 8, 1995.
3. Tad Friend, "The Untouchables," *New York*, October 16, 1995, p. 27.
4. Quoted in John H. Rhodehamel, Stephen F. Rohde, and Paul von Blum, *Foundations of Freedom: A Living History of Our Bill of Rights* (Los Angeles: Constitutional Rights Foundation, 1991), p. 95.
5. Quoted in Nicole Lemann, "Trial and Errors," *The New York Times Book Review*, March 3, 1996.
6. Jeffrey Rosen, "Bad Noose," *The New Republic*, October 4, 1993.
7. Richard Parker, "What Happens When O. J. Gets Off? The Coming Legal Backlash," *The New Republic*, March 20, 1995.
8. Parker.

Chapter 5

1. Quoted in Marc A. Franklin, *The First Amendment and the Fourth Estate* (Mineola, NY: Foundation Press, 1981), p. 374.
2. ABC poll information cited in Dan Hulbert, "Television and Radio," *The Americana Annual 1996*, (Danbury, CT: Grolier, 1996), p. 533.
3. Mark Clayton, "Canada's 'O. J.' Trial Won't Be Media Circus," *The Christian Science Monitor*, May 18, 1995.
4. Clayton.
5. *Gannett Co. v. DePasquale* (443 U.S. 368), cited in Franklin, p. 388.
6. *Nebraska Press Ass'n v. Stuart* (427 U.S. 539), cited in Franklin, p. 379.
7. Kenneth Jost, "Judges Should Gag the 'Gag Order'," *The Christian Science Monitor*, August 5, 1991.
8. Curtis D. MacDougall, *Newsroom Problems and Policies* (New York: Dover Publications, 1963), p. 380.
9. Quoted in MacDougall, p. 379.

10. "Ito Defends Camera's Role in Simpson Murder Trial," *Chicago Tribune*, October 24, 1995.
11. Rikki J. Klieman, "But a Camera in the Courtroom Should Not Take the Blame," *Chicago Tribune*, October 10, 1995.

Chapter 6

1. Quoted in John H. Rhodehamel, Stephen F. Rohde, and Paul von Blum, *Foundations of Freedom: A Living History of Our Bill of Rights* (Los Angeles: Constitutional Rights Foundation, 1991), p. 97.
2. Jan Hoffman, "Conviction Reversal Bolsters Pataki in Fight Against Court," *The New York Times*, June 13, 1996.
3. Don Terry, "After 18 Years in Prison, 3 Are Cleared of Murders," *The New York Times*, July 3, 1996.
4. Otis and Adams quoted in Robert E. Bauman, "Congress and the Exclusionary Rule: Would Killing the Exclusionary Rule Repeal the Fourth Amendment—Or Restore It?" *National Review*, May 15, 1995, p. 58.
5. Morgan O. Reynolds, "Why Stop Halfway?" *National Review*, May 15, 1995, p. 59.
6. Bauman.
7. Jeffrey Rosen, "Search and Seize: Republican Legal Onslaught II," *The New Republic*, March 27, 1995, p. 12.
8. Bauman.
9. Rhodehamel, et al., p. 94.
10. Jeffrey Rosen, "Bad Noose," *The New Republic*, October 4, 1993.
11. Quoted in Sam Howe Verhovek, "When Justice Shows Its Darker Side," *The New York Times*, January 1995.
12. Terry.

Chapter 7

1. Quoted in Jerry Adler, "Bloodied But Unbowed," *Newsweek*, April 3, 1995, p. 54.

2. Jean Sands, "'Someone We Love Was Murdered'," *The Litchfield County Times*, February 2, 1996.
3. Sands.
4. Adler.
5. *The New Republic*, April 17, 1995.
6. Adler.
7. William Glaberson, "Jersey Court to Decide Limits of Victim's Right to Address Jury," *The New York Times*, June 11, 1996.
8. *The New Republic*, April 17, 1995.
9. Adler.
10. Glaberson.

Chapter 8

1. William Pitt, speech in the British House of Commons, January 9, 1770.
2. Norman Mailer, "Black and White Justice," *New York*, October 16, 1996, p. 29.
3. Richard Parker, "What Happens When O. J. Gets Off? The Coming Legal Backlash," *The New Republic*, March 20, 1995.
4. Mailer.
5. Jacob Weisberg, "The Truth Card," *New York*, October 16, 1995, p. 33.

Further Reading

Abramson, Jeffrey. *We the Jury: The Jury System and the Ideal of Democracy.* New York: Basic Books, 1994.

Adler, Stephen J. *The Jury: Trial and Error in the American Courtroom.* New York: Times Books, 1994.

Darden, Christopher A., with Jess Walter. *In Contempt.* New York: ReganBooks/HarperCollins, 1996.

Dershowitz, Alan M. *Reasonable Doubts: The O. J. Simpson Case and the Criminal Justice System.* New York: Simon & Schuster, 1996.

Elias, Stephen, ed. *Legal Breakdown: 40 Ways to Fix Our Legal System.* Berkeley, CA: Nolo Press, 1990.

Meltzer, Milton. *The Bill of Rights: How We Got It and What It Means.* New York: Crowell, 1990.

Neely, Richard. *Why Courts Don't Work.* New York: McGraw-Hill, 1983.

Rhodehamel, John H., Stephen F. Rohde, and Paul von Blum. *Foundations of Freedom: A Living History of Our Bill of Rights.* Los Angeles: Constitutional Rights Foundation, 1991.

Stencel, Sandra, ed. "The Jury System," *CQ Researcher*, Nov. 10, 1995. Washington, D.C.: Congressional Quarterly.

Uelmen, Gerald F. *Lessons from the Trial: The People v. O. J. Simpson.* Kansas City, MO: Andrews and McMeel, 1996.

Wishman, Seymour. *Anatomy of a Jury: The System on Trial.* New York: Times Books, 1986.

Zerman, Melvyn Bernard. *Beyond a Reasonable Doubt: Inside the American Jury System.* New York: Crowell, 1981.

Index

Page numbers in *italics* refer to illustrations.

Adams, John, 78
Adler, Stephen J., 32, 38
Adversary system, 96-97
African Americans (*see* Racial bias)
Alschuler, Alvin, 46, 48
American Bar Association, 71, 80, 82
Appeals, 20-21, 76, 77, 82-84
Arraignment, 18
Arrest rates, 12
Arrest warrant, 18

Bail, 19, 81
excessive, 17
Bailey, F. Lee, 56
Bar association ethics, 68-69

Bernardo, Paul, 64
Bill of Rights, 13, 15-17, 63, 77
Bills of attainder, 14
Black, Hugo L., 52, 60, 62
Brennan, William, 67
Burger, Warren E., 63
Burr, Aaron, 65-66
Butler, Paul, 47-48

Cable News Network (CNN), 63
Cameras in court, 73-74
Canadian courts, 64-65
Chiraldi, Vincent, 45
Civil cases, process of, 21-22
Civil-law tradition, 38
Civil rights movement, 46
Clark, Tom C., 75
Clinton, Bill, 56
Closing arguments, 20

Cochran, Johnnie, 48, 56, *57*
Confessions, 79
Constitution of the United States, 13-17, 28, 29, 81, 82, 94
 First Amendment, 63, 65, 95
 Fourth Amendment, 15, 77, 78, 80, 81
 Fifth Amendment, 15
 Sixth Amendment, 13, 15-16, 63, 90, 95
 Seventh Amendment, 16-17
 Eighth Amendment, 17
 Fourteenth Amendment, 17
Consulting, jury, 32-33, 56, 58
Contingency basis, 22, 61
Conviction rates, 12
Cosby, William, 28
Counsel, right to, 16, 59-60
Court-appointed lawyers, 62
Court TV, 63, 74
Criminal cases, process of, 18-21
Cross-examination, 20
Cruel and unusual punishment, 17
Cuervo, Fernando, 75

Death penalty, 83-84, 93

Death Row prisoners, 77, 82
Defendants' rights, 12, 75-84, 89, 95
Defense attorneys, 20, 35, 36, 52, 53, 56, *57*, 58, 68-69, 71
DeLorean, John, 53
Dershowitz, Alan, 56, 60
Dieter, Richard C., 84
Discovery, 22
Double jeopardy, 15
Douglas, Carl, 56, *57*
"Dream team" legal defense, 52, 53, 56, *57*, 58
Drug laws, 44-45
Due process of law, 15, 17, 95
Duran, Francisco Martin, 56

Eighth Amendment to the U.S. Constitution, 17
English law, 24-25, 38, 65-67, 89
Equal protection under law, 17
Evidence, 12, 20, 35, 36
Exclusionary rule, 77-80, 89
Expert testimony, 36, 58
Ex post facto laws, 14

Federal court system, 14, 17, 18
Federal district courts, 18

Felonies, 17
Ferguson, Colin, 90, 92
Ferguson trial, 90, *91*, 92, 93
Fifth Amendment to the U.S. Constitution, 15
Filing fees, 22
First Amendment to the U.S. Constitution, 63, 65, 95
"Founded suspicion," 76
Fourteenth Amendment to the U.S. Constitution, 17
Fourth Amendment to the U.S. Constitution, 15, 77, 78, 80, 81
Free speech, 28
Fuhrman, Mark, *49*

Gag orders, 68
General Accounting Office, 80
George III, king of England, 77
Gideon, Clarence Earl, 58-60, *59*
Gideon v. *Wainwright* (1963), 58-60
Goldman, Ron, 11, 87
Grand jury, 19
Guilty plea, 18
Guilty verdict, 20

Habeas corpus, writ of, 14, 81-83
Hamilton, Andrew, 28

Hauptmann, Bruno Richard, 69, *70*
Homolka, Karla, 64
Hoover, J. Edgar, 71-72

Impact statements, 90, *91*, 92-94
Indictment, 19
Information (document), 18
Ito, Lance, 71, 73

Japanese Americans, 82
Judges, 35, 39, 71
Jury system, 23-40
    compensation, 33
    consulting, 32-33, 56, 58
    history of, 24-28
    media influence, 65-66
    nullification, 29, 47
    pools, 29-30, 39, 45, 46
    race and, 45-47
    reforms proposed, 39-40
    selection process, 11, 19-20, 29-30, *31*, 32-33, 39
    sequestration, *34*, 35, 40, 97
    trial complexity and, 35-36
Jury trial, right to, 9, 14, 16

Kennedy, Edward, 53
King, Rodney, 41, 43-44

King trial, 41, *42*, 44
Klieman, Rikki J., 74

Lawmen, 24, 25
Legal Aid Society, 60
Legal fees, 22, 56, 61
Legal Services Corporation, 61
Lincoln, Abraham, 82
Lindbergh, Charles, 69
Lindbergh kidnapping trial, 69, *70*, 71, 73
Local (municipal) court system, 17
Long Island Railroad shootings, 90, *91*, 92
Los Angeles Police Department, 41, 43-44
Los Angeles riots (1992), 41

Mailer, Norman, 96, 97
Mapp v. *Ohio* (1961), 79
Marcos, Ferdinand, 53
Marcos, Imelda, 53
Marshall, John, 65-66
McVeigh, Timothy, 68
Mead, William, 25
Media coverage, 11, 12, 63-74
Menendez, Erik, 36, *37*
Menendez, Lyle, 36, *37*
Menendez trial, 36, *37*, 73
Miranda, Ernesto, 79
"Miranda" rights, 79
Misdemeanors, 17

Money (*see* Wealth, advantages of)

National Organization for Victim Assistance (NOVA), 89
New Republic, The, 92-93
New-York Weekly Journal, *26*, 28
Nichols, Terry, 68
Nolo contendere plea, 18
Note-taking, 35, 36
Not guilty plea, 18
Not guilty verdict, 20

Oath-helpers, 24, 25
Oklahoma bombing trial, 68
Otis, James, 78
Out-of-court settlement, 22

Page, Clarence, 51, 52
Parents of Murdered Children and Other Survivors of Homicide Victims, 86
Parker, Richard, 62, 96
Parole, 43
Penn, William, 25
Peremptory challenge, 30, 32
Pitt, William, 95
Plea bargaining, 19, 60, 67, 90
Pleas, 18
Preliminary hearing, 19
Press, freedom of, 65, 95

Pretrial hearing, 19, 21, 67
Pretrial publicity, 67-69
Prison population, 43
Probable cause, 15, 77
Probation, 43
Pro bono, 58, 61
Prosecution, 20, 35, 36, 68, 71
Public defender, 18, 60

Racial bias, 11-12, 41-51, 97
   jury system and, 45-47
   verdict and, 47-48, 51
Rieger, Sam, 85-87
Rieger, Wanda, 85
Riot laws, 89
Roughing It (Twain), 32

Saldivar, Yolanda, 55
Scheck, Barry, 56
Search and seizure, 15, 77-81
Selena, 55
Sentencing, 20
Sequestration, jury, *34*, 35, 40, 97
Seventh Amendment to the U.S. Constitution, 16-17
Shadow jury, 33
Shapiro, Robert, 41, 56, *57*
Simpson, Nicole Brown, *10*, 11, 33, 87
Simpson, O. J., *10*, 11, 43, *57*, 63, 87

Simpson trial, 11, 23, 35, 38, 40, 41, 43, 48, *49*, *50*, 51-53, 56, *57*, 60, 63, 64, 69, 71, *72*, 73-74, 96
Singleton, Cornelius, 61
Sixth Amendment to the U.S. Constitution, 13, 15-16, 63, 90, 95
Smart, Pamela, 53, 55
Smith, Susan, *55*, 55-56
Smith, William Kennedy, 53, *54*, 68
Speech, freedom of, 28
State constitutions, 17
State court system, 17
Stein, John, 85, 90
Strayhorn, Earl, 48
Supreme Court of the United States, 29
   on appeal process, 82
   cases heard by, 21
   exclusionary rule and, 78-80
   on impact statements, 93
   on pretrial hearing publicity, 67
   on right to legal counsel, 58-60
   on women and minorities on juries, 45-46

Till, Emmett, 47
Treason, definition of, 14
Turriago, Leonardo, 75-76

Twain, Mark, 23, 32
Tyson, Mike, 48

Unreasonable searches and
seizures, 15, 77-79

Venues, changing, 68
Verdicts, 20
    racial bias and, 47-48,
    51
Victims' rights, 12, 85-95
Vikings, 24
Voir dire process, 30, 66
von Bulow, Claus, 53, 60

Warrantless searches and
seizures, 75-81

Warrants, 15
Wealth, advantages of, 12,
    22, 52-62, 96, 97
Weeks v. *United States*
    (1914), 78
Weisberg, Jacob, 97
Williams, Dennis, 77,
    83
Witnesses, 16, 20
Wollan, Laurin A., Jr., 83-
    84
Women, jury duty and, 45,
    46
Writs of assistance, 77-78

Zenger, John Peter, 26-27,
    28